The Life, Times, and Influence of Alexander William Doniphan

Alexander Doniphan Committee

THE LIFE, TIMES, AND INFLUENCE OF

Alexander William Doniphan

ALEXANDER
DONIPHAN COMMITTEE

Copyright © 2020 Alexander Doniphan Committee. All rights reserved. No part of this publication may be reproduced, stored in a retrieval system, stored in a database and / or published in any form or by any means, electronic, mechanical, photocopying, recording or otherwise, without the prior written permission of the publisher.

To request permissions, contact the publisher at storycenter@mymcpl.org.

ISBN 978-1-942337-20-1

Firstpaperback edition December 2020.

Edited by Valerie Abbott of Writing Help KC.
Cover art and layout by Lori Garcia of Lori Garcia Studios.

WOODNEATH PRESS

Woodneath Press
8900 NE Flintlock Road
Kansas City, MO 64157
816.883.4774 | MyStoryCenter.org
A program of The Story Center at
Mid-Continent Public Library

The Alexander W. Doniphan Community Service & Leadership Award Committee

The Alexander W. Doniphan Community Service & Leadership Award Committee is dedicated to preserving the legacy of Alexander Doniphan and honoring those in the community who exemplify his outstanding characteristics and personal commitments in one or more of the diverse components of his life, namely Education, Jurisprudence, Statesmanship, Patriotism in Defense of Country, and Integrity in Business. This book is a gift from the Alexander W. Doniphan Committee to the State of Missouri as we commemorate the bicentennial of Missouri's statehood in 2021.

John A. Dillingham and Cynthia McDavitt, Co-Chairs

Rodney Ames, Robert Arter, Raymond Brock Jr., Sheryl Gallagher, Kurt Graham, Laurie Jacobus, Jeremiah J. Morgan, Steven V. Potter, W. Christian Sizemore & Eric Zahnd

Contributors

Alexander L. Baugh, " Alexander W. Doniphan on National Television: The NBC Nationwide Telecast of Profiles in Courage" Copyright © 2020

Allen Jones, "Alexander W. Doniphan: American Xenophon" Copyright © 2020

Caldwell County (MO) Commission, " History of Caldwell County" Copyright © 2016

David W. Jackson, "Colonel Alexander William Doniphan: Trials on the Missouri Frontier" Copyright © 2020

J. Bradley Pace, "Mr. Doniphan Goes to Court" Copyright © 2020

Jeremiah J. Morgan, " Alexander W. Doniphan: The Trial of His Life" Copyright © 2020

John Dillingham, "Civil War Roundtable: Alexander W. Doniphan" Copyright © 2020

Kathleen Bird, "Pick a Side: Doniphan's Role in Missouri's Loyalty to the Union" Copyright © 2020

Kelvin Crow, "Alexander W. Doniphan: Fort Leavenworth and Mexican American War" Copyright © 2020

NGP Newspapers, "Jack "Miles" Ventimiglia" Copyright © 2020

Steven V. Potter, "Influential Missourian Alexander Doniphan" Copyright © 2020

Susan Easton Black, "Alexander W. Doniphan: In Defense of Mormons" Copyright © 2020

Taryn Duffy, " Sentiments of Honor" Copyright © 2020

W. Christian Sizemore, " Alexander Doniphan: A Path to Follow" Copyright © 2020

Table of Contents

Foreword xi
Foreword xv

The Life of Alexander William Doniphan

Chapter 1 : The Settlement of the Peculiar People in
Jackson County and Subsequent Expulsion,
Kansas City Daily Journal, Sunday, June 12, 1881 3

Chapter 2 : Alexander W. Doniphan, 1808–1887 Soldier,
Lawyer, and Orator, *Floyd Calvin Shoemaker* 13

Chapter 3 : Colonel Alexander William Doniphan: Trials
on the Missouri Frontier, *David W. Jackson* 27

Chapter 4 : Alexander W. Doniphan: In Defense of
Mormons, *Dr. Susan Easton Black* 55

Chapter 5 : Alexander W. Doniphan, Fort Leavenworth
and Mexican American War, *Kelvin Crow* 87

Chapter 6 : Alexander W. Doniphan "American Xenophon,"
Allen Jones 93

Chapter 7 : Music Perhaps Unheard in 150 Years Plays
Sunday, *Jack "Miles" Ventimiglia* 109

The Times of Alexander William Doniphan

Chapter 8 : Pick a Side: Doniphan's Role in Missouri's
Loyalty to the Union, *Kathleen Bird, JD* 115

Table of Contents Cont.

Chapter 9 : Mr. Doniphan Goes to Court, *J. Bradley Pace*............137

Chapter 10 :The Trial of His Life, *Jeremiah J. Morgan*............161

The Influence of Alexander William Doniphan

Chapter 11 :Alexander W. Doniphan on National Television: The NBC Nationwide Telecast of Profiles in Courage, *Alexander L. Baugh*............185

Chapter 12 :Influential Missourian Alexander Doniphan, *Steven V. Potter*............203

Chapter 13 :The History of Caldwell County, *Caldwell County Missouri Website*............207

Chapter 14 :Camp Names and What's in Them, *John Walker Harrington*............215

Chapter 15 :Sentiments of Honor, *Taryn Duffy*............223

Chapter 16 :Alexander Doniphan Marches to Truman Library, *John Dillingham*............231

Chapter 17 :Civil War Roundtable: Alexander W. Doniphan, *John Dillingham*............237

Chapter 18 :Alexander Doniphan—A Path to Follow, *Dr. W. Christian Sizemore*............249

Epilogue............255

Image Gallery............259

Foreword

John C. Danforth

There's a word that's recently gained a lot of currency in America. The word is "tribal." You see it all the time. David Brooks has featured it in newspaper columns. Law professor Amy Chua has written about it in a book called Political Tribes. Here in a nutshell is her point.

Everyone in America today feels threatened. African Americans fear that their children will be shot by police. Mexicans are threatened with deportation. Muslims are told their religion should be barred from the country. Women are abused by workplace predators. Poor whites feel left behind by a country that calls them "trash." Religious conservatives are threatened by popular culture. Amy Chua notes that when people feel threatened they retreat into tribalism, a hostile world of us against them.

We think of divisive tribalism as a new phenomenon in America, and it has certainly been exacerbated by current rhetoric, both political and academic. But the life and times of Alexander Doniphan tell us that tribalism in America has a long history, bloodier than what we have today.

Doniphan gained fame in 1838 during a largely forgotten crisis in Northwest Missouri known as the Mormon War. Mormons were greatly feared at that time for their growing political and economic power, and it became politically popular to persecute them. They were expelled from Jackson County, and they moved from one county to another in search of safety. Governor Lilburn Boggs ordered their removal from the state or extermination. Fighting broke out between Mormons and the state militia, and 22 people were killed. Joseph Smith and other Mormons were captured, tried by a kangaroo court, and convicted of treason. Alexander Doniphan, a brigadier general, was ordered by his military superior to execute the Mormons. He flatly refused to do so, saying that their execution would amount to "cold blooded murder." Doniphan subsequently defended the Mormons at their trial in Liberty.

As Amy Chua has said, when people feel threatened, they resort to tribalism. That's what happened in Missouri more than 180 years ago. Non-Mormons were afraid that their farms would be taken from them, that they would lose political power, so they turned against the Mormons to the point of bloodshed.

And those in power, the politicians, the governor, the state militia pandered to the fear and sided with the mob.

That was then. This is now. It's an age old political tactic to play to tribal instincts, to turn us against them, and it persists today.

But at our best, we Americans have known that it cannot be us against them. It must be we the people. We must be one nation indivisible. And it's our duty as Americans to stand against all who would divide us and to hold ourselves together.

So when politicians encourage tribalism, when they say we should act against Muslims or Mexicans or any other group, it's up to us to follow the example of Alexander Doniphan when he refused the order to execute the Mormons—to insist that we're not going to do that, we're not going to be like that. We come from many different lands, and we are of different races and religions, and we are all Americans. That's what makes us great, and that's what makes us proud.

John C. Danforth is a highly respected politician, attorney, diplomat and ordained Episcopal priest from St. Louis, Missouri. He served the people in many ways including as Ambassador to the United Nations, United States Senator, Missouri Attorney General, and Special Counsel to the U.S. Justice Department.

THE WILL OF MISSOURI: THE LIFE, TIMES, & INFLUENCE OF ALEXANDER WILLIAM DONIPHAN

Foreword

The Missouri Bicentennial and Community History

Steven V. Potter

At the very core of the human experience is the story. For whatever the reason, stories appeal to us, speak to us, and record our experiences. Stories can do so much. They can entertain, they can inform, they can create a shared experience. Any time I talk about Mid-Continent Public Library's Story Center Program, I share this observation. Interestingly, this anthology shares all these traits, but it is so much more.

For several years, Jeremiah Morgan and I discussed the idea of developing a writing project about Alexander Doniphan. For many reasons, he and I both believe that Doniphan was an incredible man of his time. As time marched on and despite the efforts of many, people did not know Doniphan's story. Jeremiah and I kept talking about this project with our friends and fellow admirers, John Dillingham and Chris Sizemore. The four of us are part of an association dedicated to preserving Doniphan's legacy and recognizing community members who exhibit his exceptional traits. The association has many projects in mind, and we had discussed the idea of a writing project for a long time. But the conversation rarely got beyond a conversation. It was the germ of an idea that needed a catalyst to propel this project from idea to reality.

One very important development in the life of this project was timing. As fate would have it, these discussions were happening just before the 200th anniversary of Missouri's admission as the twenty-fourth state in the Union. The Missouri Bicentennial would provide the momentum to propel the project ahead. Michael Sweeny from the State Historical Society of Missouri was reaching out to Missouri's public libraries to collect ideas on how Missouri might celebrate this very special anniversary. He and I had several conversations about this important event and how Mid-Continent Public Library might be able to help promote the State Historical Society's efforts.

How do communities celebrate special anniversaries? Some communities established parks, statues, or other public amenities. Some communities created time capsules, dedicated historical markers or other types monuments. Mr. Sweeny and I were talking about past efforts like those previously mentioned. I remembered stories people told me about aging roadside historical markers to celebrate the State Historical Society's centennial. Time marched on and the interstate highway system was established. Eventually the attraction and necessity of roadside parks waned. What seemed like a great way to celebrate an important anniversary a little more than fifty years ago, now was an obligation for future generations to fund and to maintain. I was certain that the first proposals would be to create monuments like those mentioned before. But what if there was a different way to celebrate? What if there was a way for people to celebrate today and pass on a gift for tomorrow? Most importantly, what if that gift was truly a gift and not an obligation?

Considering the conversations that I had with my friends and with Mr. Sweeny, I proposed a community history project to chronical the life, the times and the influence of Alexander Doniphan to celebrate Missouri's bicentennial. This project would serve as a model for other Missouri communities. The concept is simple. A steering community within a community will identify a topic; a special person, place or event that helps to uniquely define that community. That steering committee will approach people from the community and ask them to contribute to this story. How one contributes is not important. The contribution could be an essay, photographs, a drawing, a poem, or even a song. But the idea is for the community to tell a story about something that uniquely defines that community by exploring the subject's history (or life), the times in which the subject occurred, and the influence (or presumed influence) of the subject over time. In the end, the community would record a contemporary account of something important. Perhaps even more important, the result would be a manuscript. Something that can be stored and maintained with little effort and without burden to future generations.

This project serves as a template and a model for other communities to celebrate Missouri's bicentennial. The State Historical Society endorsed this project as one of the many projects to help celebrate Missouri's history.

THE WILL OF MISSOURI: THE LIFE, TIMES, & INFLUENCE OF ALEXANDER WILLIAM DONIPHAN

The Life of Alexander William Doniphan

CHAPTER 1

The Settlement of the Peculiar People in Jackson County and Subsequent Expulsion.

Kansas City Daily Journal, Sunday, June 12, 1881

During the summer of 1881, the Kansas City Daily Journal published a series of articles regarding the expulsion of members of The Church of Jesus Christ of Latter-day Saints (commonly referred to as Mormons) from Jackson County. The following document published Sunday, June 12, 1881, is the interview with Alexander W. Doniphan, friend and attorney to the Saints.

Chapter Page Image: Taken between 1844 and 1860, this image of Alexander W. Doniphan was taken by famed photographer, Matthew Brady. -- *Brady, M. (1992). Alexander William Doniphan, head-and-shoulders portrait, facing front [Photograph found in Daguerreotype collection, Library of Congress, Washington]. Retrieved July, 2020, from www.loc.gov/item/2004663929 (Originally photographed circa 1844)*

There is probably no man in western Missouri who is better acquainted with the various causes of the difficulties between the citizens of Jackson and Caldwell Counties and the Mormons during the years of 1833 and 1838 than Gen. Alexander W. Doniphan, then a resident of Clay County, but now of Richmond, Ray County, Mo., and there is, perhaps, no one who took such an active part in the events of those years who can now look back and relate the history of those troubles as dispassionately as he can. In view of these facts, a representative of the Journal called upon Gen. Doniphan at his rooms at the Hudgins' house at Richmond, for the purpose of interviewing him upon the subject.[1] The general, after learning the object of the visit, seemed very willing to communicate all he knew in regard to the history of the Mormon troubles, and after a few introductory remarks, related the following:

> I came to Missouri in 1830, and located in Lexington, where I lived until April 1833, when I removed to Liberty, Clay County. The Mormons came to Jackson County in 1830, and I met Oliver Cowdery, John Whitmer, and Christian Whitmer, three of the Elders, in Independence, during the spring of 1831. Peter Whitmer was a tailor and I employed him to make me a suit of clothes.

What kind of people were the Mormons?

> They were northern people, who, on account of their declining to own slaves and their denunciation of the system of slavery, were termed "Free Soilers." The majority of them were intelligent, industrious and law-abiding citizens, but there were some ignorant, simple minded fanatics among them, whom the prophet said would steal. Soon after they

came to Jackson County, they established a newspaper at Independence called the Morning and Evening Star, edited by W.W. Phelps, in which they published their peculiar tenets and pretended revelations in which they set forth that they had been sent to Jackson County by divine Providence and that they, as a church were to possess the whole of the country, which then embraced what is now Jackson, Cass, and Bates Counties. These assumptions were evidently made use of for the purpose of exciting the jealousy of persons of other religious denominations and the more ignorant portions of the community. This of course caused hard feelings between them and the people of the county, but I think the real objections to the Mormons were their denunciation of slavery, and the objections slave holders had to having so large a settlement of anti-slavery people in their midst, and also to their acquiring such a large amount of land, which then belonged to the government, and subject to pre-emption. From these and other causes, a very bitter feeling was engendered between the Mormons and citizens which culminated in the month of July, 1833, when a public meeting was held at the courthouse in Independence, at which it was resolved to tear down the Mormon printing establishment, which resolve was immediately carried out. The mob also committed numerous other outrages, the most brutal of which was the tarring and feathering of Bishop Partridge. I can't positively state who were the leaders of the mob, but it was participated in by a large number of the leading citizens of the county. The Mormons made but little if any resistance, but submitted to the inevitable, and agreed not to establish another paper, and there was an apparent tranquility existing until about the first of the following November when from imprudent conduct upon both sides, both Mormons and Gentiles—as the citizens were then called by the Mormons—seemed to arm themselves as if expecting a collision. The first clash of arms took place at Wilson's store on the Big Blue, about four miles east of Westport, about the third or fourth day of November, which resulted in several persons being killed upon both sides and several others wounded.

"In a few days after this the citizens organized and determined upon ejecting the Mormons from the county which soon after was done. During the ejectment a great many outrages were perpetrated and the Mormons were compelled to leave almost everything they possessed behind them, and it was only by a hurried flight that they saved their lives. As it was, quite a number were killed on both sides. The majority of the Mormons, after being driven from Jackson County, went to Clay County, where they were received and provided for as well as was possible by the citizens. The Mormons remained in Clay County until 1836, in an unorganized community, when it was agreed between them and the citizens of Clay and Ray Counties that if they (the Mormons) would buy out a few citizens then inhabiting what is now Caldwell County, then a part of Ray County, the balance of the land being public, they could enter it at their leisure and we would urge the legislature to create a county for them, which was done at the session of the legislature of 1836-37."

"I was a member of the legislature and drew the bill organizing Caldwell County for the Mormons exclusively, and the offices of the county were given to their people. The new county filled up very rapidly and they made great progress in agricultural and other improvements. They continued to live prosperously and tranquilly until the summer of 1838, when Joseph Smith came out from Ohio and soon after they commenced forming a settlement in Davis County, which, under their agreement, they had no right to do. This occasioned difficulties with the citizens of Davis County, and in September, 1838, a large number of citizens of Davis and adjoining counties collected with arms in the Mormon settlement called 'Adam-on-di-Ahman,' in Davis [sic] county.[2] The Mormons also gathered at the same point, and I, being at that time brigadier general of the western division of Missouri, was sent by Gov. Boggs with a regiment of Clay County militia to prevent a collision, which after being there one week, I was able to do, and left them apparently harmonious, the Mormons agreeing that they would return to Caldwell County as soon as they could take care of their crops, etc."

About one month after this new difficulties arose between the citizens and Mormons, from what causes I never knew, which culminated in the Mormons burning and sacking the Gentile towns of Millport and Gallatin, then very small villages. A few days after this a battle took place on the line between Caldwell and Ray Counties between the Mormons, under the command of Capt. Patton, and the citizens of Ray County, under command of Capt. Bogart, in which two Ray County citizens and several Mormons, including Capt. Patton, were killed. The place where the battle occurred is still known as "Bogart's Battle Ground."

Gen. Atchison, who was afterwards United States senator, was then major general of Northwest Missouri, ordered me to raise a regiment of militia from Clay, Clinton, and Platte Counties. I did so, and proceeded at once to the battleground, and the next day I received an order from Gov. [Lilburn W.] Boggs to take command of all the forces and remain in Ray County until the arrival of Gen. [John B.] Clark with the state troops. Being satisfied that the governor had overestimated the number of Mormons, I went on to Far West, county seat of Caldwell County, where all the Mormon forces were assembled. I sent for Judge King, of the circuit court, to come to my camp, and at that juncture Gen. S.D. [Samuel D.] Lucas, of Jackson County, arrived with a small number of men sent out by the governor. I opened negotiations with the Mormons by going up to their lines in person, and when Judge King came out, I consulted with him, and upon his advice, the Mormons gave up their arms and turned over to me such men as had violated the laws of the land, and those upon the other side who had done the same were arrested upon warrants issued by Judge King. It has been said that in the treaty I made with the Mormons, I stipulated that they must leave the State, under penalty of annihilation if they refused to do so. This is utterly untrue as I made no such stipulation. It is true, however, that in an order to me and other officers, Gov. Boggs used the expression "that the Mormons leave the state or be exterminated," whereas this order was entirely illegal. I paid no attention to it. In my report to Gov. Boggs, I stated to him that I had disregarded that part of his order, as the age of extermination was over, and if I attempted to remove them to some other state, it would cause additional trouble. The Mormons commenced immediately after this to move to Nauvoo, Ill., and I know nothing further about them. While the Mormons resided in Clay County, they were a peaceable, sober, industrious, and law-abiding people, and during their stay with us, not one was ever accused of a crime of any kind.

Gen. Doniphan is now in his seventy-third year, but is still hale and hearty. He is a man of fine appearance and intellect, and is well known and highly respected all over the state. He has resided in Richmond during the past several years. His statements as given above may be relied upon as strictly the truth in every particular. There are a few old citizens still living near Independence who were in this county during the troubles of 1833, whose statements will be given in the near future.[3]

Endnotes

1. The text of this interview was reprinted in various publications of the Reorganized Church of Jesus Christ of Latter-day Saints (RLDS), and was eventually added to the official *RLDS Church History*, 4, 360–62.

2. Original text said "Davis" instead of "Daviess"

3. For more on General Doniphan, see Roger Launius' 1997 *Alexander William Doniphan: Portrait of a Missouri Moderate.* The Kirksville, Missouri *Weekly Graphic,* September 28, 1883 featured a similar Doniphan interview, and the Lamoni, Iowa *Saint's Herald*, August 2, 1884 published a brief report of Reorganized LDS leaders meeting with the General. Mormon Historian George A. Smith had many laudatory things to say about Doniphan (then visiting the Utah Saints) in his discourse of May 24, 1874, which was published in the *Deseret Evening News*, June 13, 1874.

CHAPTER 2

Alexander W. Doniphan, 1808–1887 Soldier, Lawyer, and Orator[1]

Floyd Calvin Shoemaker

Originally published in 1921. This is a somewhat dated and stilted biography about Doniphan. The writing and style is not fitting for contemporary reader. However, authorship is closer to the time of the man and likely part of a Missouri centennial project.

Chapter Page Image: Alexander W. Doniphan found in the centennial work, Missouri's Hall of Fame. -- *Shoemaker, F. C. (1921). Alexander W. Doniphan, 1806-1887 : Soldier, Lawyer and Orator. In Missouri's Hall of Fame: Lives of Eminent Missourians (p. 107). Columbia, MO: Missouri Book Company.*

A people wonderful in deeds are the citizens of Missouri. Native born, nine out of ten, they are true types of the patriotic American. Missouri's first American settlers came largely from Virginia, Kentucky, Tennessee, and the two Carolinas. These pioneers were of hardy stock. They had fought Native Americans[2] and had endured the hardships of the frontier. They were born soldiers, large of frame, keen of eye, and not afraid of death. They found Missouri a wilderness, where roamed the Native Americans[3] except for a few settlements along the Mississippi River. Their first task was to blaze trails through the country, build forts and establish frontier settlements. This was hard work and took years to do. Battle with the Native Americans[4] were many. Subduing the wilderness with its dense forest and brush, its wild animals, and frequently its unhealthy climate, required courage and toil.

It was these hardships, however, that trained the pioneer Missourian to overcome all obstacles, to fear neither man or beast, and to willingly give his life for what he thought was right. It produced a race of such dauntless men as Gen Henry Dodge, who defeated the great Indian chief, Black Hawk; Kit Carson, the great guide of the West; General Richard Gentry, who with his ban of Missouri soldiers, waged war in Florida against the Seminole Indian chief, Osceola; and scores of other early heroes. Among the greatest and most renowned of these was one who came to Missouri [as] a young man, lived and married here, and whose remains today rest in Missouri soil—Col. Alexander W. Doniphan, soldier, lawyer, statesman, orator, and gentleman.

Born in Kentucky on July 9, 1808, Doniphan was the youngest of twelve children. His father died when young Doniphan was only six years old. His mother, who was a remarkable woman, gave him a fine education. He had the best of teachers and later graduated with honest honors from college.

His ambition was to be a lawyer, and he studied under several of the best lawyers in Kentucky. At the age of twenty-one, he was admitted to the bar and began to practice law.

The following year, he came and settled in Lexington, Missouri. Although only twenty-two years old, he was soon looked upon as a good lawyer. He had neither friends nor funds at first, and had to compete against some of the best lawyers in the state. Instead of being discouraged, he worked harder. It was not long until he had built up a large practice.

He moved to Liberty in 1833 and lived there thirty years. He was elected a member of the Missouri Legislature three times, although he belonged to the minority party in Missouri—the Whigs. These elections were due to his great popularity.

He married a Clay County girl, and to them were born two sons. One of Colonel Doniphan's greatest disappointments in life was the early death of these two boys. One died of accidental poisoning, the other of drowning.

Colonel Doniphan was made a brigadier general in the Missouri militia and commanded a brigade at the time of the Mormon troubles in the state. In 1846 to 1847, he led an Expedition of One Thousand Missourians during the Mexican War and returned with highest honors.

He held other public offices, with credit to himself and his country. During the Civil War, he took the side of the Union. He made his home in St. Louis for a few years, and in 1868, moved to Richmond, Missouri. His wife died in 1873. Her loss greatly depressed him with grief. For twenty-eight years, he was a member of the Christian church. On August 8, 1887, when in his eightieth year, he died at his home in Richmond. He sleeps today by his wife's side in a grave in Liberty. A fine statue of him was erected in Richmond by the State of Missouri.

The story of the life of Col. Alexander W. Doniphan is classic in Missouri history. The influence of his life was felt all over the state. His life story reveals a great man, equipped mentally and morally to conquer, but not ambitious to hold public office. His greatness is also shown in the many different lines of work he did well.

> As a lawyer, he stood in the front rank of his profession.
>
> As a statesman, he had the confidence of his people.
>
> As an orator, he was the equal of Missouri's most eloquent speakers.
>
> As a soldier, he won fame that will last forever.
>
> And as a citizen and gentleman, he was honest, courteous, and public spirited.
>
> In all these, he won distinction and served well his state.

As a lawyer, Colonel Doniphan was very successful. This was due to his fine education and his training in law. He knew literature and history—both American and English—as well as a professor. It is said that before he was twenty-five years old, he was known as a great lawyer over all Western Missouri.

Colonel Doniphan was a criminal lawyer, i.e., he took lawsuits regarding robbery, murder, and theft. He never prosecuted, but always defended the person on trial. He made the closing speech for his client, and it was then that he frequently moved men and women, juries, and judges, to tears. He could explain a law so simply that even a schoolboy or girl could understand it. He reasoned everything out accurately. His speeches were never prepared beforehand but delivered extemporaneously. These speeches won the praise of even his opponents. His language was beautiful and his gestures graceful. He also had a magnetic presence that drew people to him. He never talked long sometimes his speech before a jury was only fifteen minutes in length.

One of his most famous cases was the Turnham case. In this case, he defended the son of Major Turnham who was accused of crime. After Colonel Doniphan had finished, Major Turnham was asked what he thought of it. He answered:

"Sir, Aleck Doniphan spoke only forty minutes, [but] he said everything."

It is one of the regrettable things that few of Colonel Doniphan's speeches have been preserved.

As a statesman, Doniphan achieved distinction. He was not ambitious to hold public office, but his sense of duty forced him to accept several. He did this at a loss in money, for he had to give up his profitable law practice. He was able and honest as a statesman and was highly regarded by all.

He went to Washington, D.C., in 1861 to attend a celebrated conference of men from other states. Here he met President Lincoln. On being introduced, President Lincoln said:

"And this is the Colonel Doniphan who made the wild march against the Comanches (Native Americans)[5] and Mexicans! You are the only man I ever met who in appearance, come up to my expectations."

As an orator, Colonel Doniphan was one of the most eloquent in Missouri. Senator David R. Atchison, who had heard [Daniel] Webster, [Henry] Clay, [Thomas Hart] Benton, and other American speakers said:

"I knew Aleck Doniphan well, intimately, since 1830; and I tell you, sir, when he was at his best, I heard him climb higher than any of them."

Colonel Doniphan's appearance was imposing. In height, he was six feet and four inches. He had a fine head and his forehead was high. His eyes were hazel and his lips always smiling. When young his complexion was fair and his hair sandy.

Colonel Doniphan told a friend that he never began a speech without feeling bashful. Many great orators have said the same thing about themselves. Col. D.C. Allen of Liberty, knew Doniphan well, and this is what he says

> What an orator we was! Men who had been in Congress used to say that Webster and Clay could not sway men as could old Alex Doniphan. He may have been bashful before he began, but once under way he was on fire. The whole man was like a flame. His burning eyes, his gestures, his tall figure—

everything about was like fire. I think perhaps I cannot give you a better idea of him than to tell you what an old woodsman, Adam K. McClintock, told me once. He was describing a barbecue on the Clear Fork of Fishing River at a place called Hawkin's Mill. McClintock, a young man, was helping serve the barbecue and at first he paid no particular attention to the speaking. There were several speakers.

Charmed Birds and Squirrels

"Finally it came around to Doniphan," the woodsman said, "and instantly there was a great rush of people from all around to the speakers' stand. At the very first, I paid no particular attention to it. As he went on, he charmed not only the people, but the birds and the wild animals. I discovered that the trees around the speakers' stand were all full of birds and squirrels, chattering and barking away. He even charmed the birds and the squirrels out of their lairs. I never saw such an affect produced on people as he made that day. He was young, very tall and splendid looking with a voice very keen, which rang through the woods, and an eye that flashed lightning."

While Colonel Doniphan won fame as a lawyer, statesman, and orator, it was as a soldier that he attracted the attention of the nation. No Missourian has a more permanent [sic] place in history than he. It was as a soldier that he won greatest distinction.

His first military campaign was in 1838 and was against the Mormons at Far West, in Caldwell County, Missouri. He commanded the First Missouri Brigade and was ordered to proceed to the storm center of the Mormon troubles. A battle was expected, but Colonel Doniphan induced the Mormons to surrender their arms, give up their leaders, and leave the state. So ended successfully and without the loss of a man on either side, his first campaign.

The second and last campaign of Colonel Doniphan was made in from 1846 to 1847 during the Mexican War. This campaign was the famous Doniphan's Expedition of One Thousand Missourians. Th expedition was completed in twelve months, during which time the men traveled four thousand miles by land and two thousand five hundred miles by sea. It returned laden with spoils and lost less than one hundred men.

Doniphan's Expeditions of One Thousand Missourians is classic in history. It left its base of supplies at Fort Leavenworth, Kansas, crossed the plains of Kansas and Colorado, and then the mountains and deserts of New Mexico and northern old Mexico. Its path was contested by bands of Indians, large Mexican armies, and by nature's weapons of heat and cold, hunger and thirst. It conquered two powerful tribes of Indians, won two battles against the Mexicans where the Missourians were outnumbered four to one, and subdued several hundred thousand hostile Mexicans. It captured many cities, three capitals, and four Mexican states.

The route of the Expedition was from Fort Leavenworth to Santa Fe, New Mexico. From Santa Fe, the army went into the mountains and conquered some Indian tribes. The men had received no pay for their service since leaving home, and their clothes were in bad condition. Their spirits were high, however, and they were full of fight.

Leaving Santa Fe in December 1846, they marched to the Rio Grande River. The cold wind and snow on the desert caused the men to suffer greatly. They had neither winter clothing nor tents. On part of the march, they were without water for ninety miles.

They reached the Brazito river, a small stream, on Christmas day and prepared to camp. Colonel Doniphan sought recreation over a game of cards. He was playing with his officers for a stake. The winner was to have a fine Mexican horse, which had been captured earlier in the day. But the game was not to be finished. A messenger stood before the Colonel:

"There is a big cloud of dust to the south, which must be the Mexicans approaching," he said.

"Then we must stop the game long enough to whip the Mexicans," Colonel Doniphan said rising. "But remember, I have the biggest score, and we will play it out as soon as the battle is finished."

The troops under Colonel Doniphan were soon looking into the fire-spitting muzzles of the enemy's [sic] guns. The Missourians did not fire. They waited. It was the order of their commander.

The fire of the Mexicans grew fiercer. But the Missourians only waited the order to fire. At last it was given. The Mexicans had reached within one hundred and fifty yards of the Missourians when they were fired upon. The enemy was checked, the horses reared upon their haunches, and many of the Mexicans fled in panic. The others were soon defeated by the keen aim of the Missourians. Over fifty Mexicans were killed and one hundred were wounded, while only seven Missourians were injured, none fatally. The victors obtained many spoils in horses, ammunition, cannon, and food. That Christmas night, Doniphan's soldiers celebrated their victory, known in history as the Battle of Brazito.

From Brazito, Colonel Doniphan marched to El Paso, which he captured. From there, he entered northern Mexico and won against four thousand Mexicans in the Battle of Sacramento. He then captured cities in northern Mexico. His troops embarked on ship for New Orleans and came on to St. Louis. At home, they were received with dinners and speeches. Missouri was indeed proud of Colonel Doniphan and his One Thousand Missourians.

As a citizen, Colonel Doniphan represented the best and highest ideals. His private and social live was perfect. He was a loving husband, a just and liberal father. He was a pleasant neighbor, honorable in all his dealings with men. He was generous and helped many young men with his advice and money. He was a true friend of education. He was often seen visiting the grade and the high schools.

He encouraged the children. For years, he served on the school board in Liberty, and in 1854, when at the height of his Mexican War fame, he accepted the humble position of commissioner of superintendent of the public schools of Clay County. He said he ought to do so because the people of the county had done everything they could for him. He held this office one year and brought honor to it and to himself by establishing the first Teachers' Institute held in Missouri.

Colonel Doniphan's greatest work for education was his securing the location of William Jewell College at Liberty. When this question came before the General Baptist Convention, the principal rivals for the school were Boonville, Columbia, Fayette, and Liberty. Few thought that Liberty had a chance of getting the college because it was situated so near the western frontier. Boonville, the meeting place of the Convention, had certain advantages. Fayette was also favored. Columbia had the best chance since it was the home of Dr. William Jewell. Doctor Jewell offered a bonus of $10,000 in land if Columbia was given the college.

Clay County was represented by Colonel Doniphan, who was not even a member of the Baptist church. Colonel Doniphan spoke for Liberty and by his eloquence, won the college for his town. Colonel Doniphan saw that Dr. William Jewell was deeply disappointed and so he arose and proposed to the Convention that the college by named "William Jewell." This was agreed to, and in gratitude, Doctor Jewell publicly donated the $10,000 in land.

Colonel Alexander W. Doniphan was a conquering genius. He was a friend of education and religion. He was an orator and a lawyer of note. His career as a soldier, while brief, will ever live. He was a kind father and husband, a true neighbor and friend, and a model gentleman in all things.

Endnotes

1. (Shoemaker 1921)

2. The term "Native Americans" replaced the original text of "Indians."

3. The term "Native Americans" replaced the original text of "savage Indians."

4. The term "Native Americans" replaced the original text of "Indians."

5. The term "Native Americans" replaced the original text of "Indians."

CHAPTER 3

Colonel Alexander William Doniphan: Trials on the Missouri Frontier

David W. Jackson

An history of the life of Alexander Doniphan. Of benefit and interest in this article is the family history and genealogy research of Doniphan and his ancestors. In addition, there is record of Doniphan's slaveholding and ownership in this article.

Chapter Page Image: Final resting place of Alexander W. Doniphan in Liberty, Missouri. -- Anderson, Valerie. (2020, April 29). Doniphan Gravesite [Photograph]. *Giving River Images, Liberty, MO.*

Alexander William Doniphan's contributions to American military history—his contributions in the Mormon and Mexican Wars—is extensively studied and easily discoverable. This feature focuses as much as possible on the personal, family, and professional life and times of one of Clay County (and later, Ray County), Missouri's prominent citizens.

Doniphan's lifelong career as a defense lawyer was punctuated with illustrious military service in the footsteps of his father, a Revolutionary War patriot. He also held positions as a local school superintendent, community banker, and while not a politician, served a handful of terms as a Missouri state lawmaker.

Alexander William Doniphan was born in Mason County, Kentucky, on July 9, 1808. He was the youngest of eight children of Joseph Doniphan (born in 1757 in King George County, Virginia–12 Mar 1814) and Anne Fowke (Smith) Doniphan (1768–post 1814).[1]

Mary Anne Doniphan
b. 1785 - Fauquier County, Virginia

Thomas Smith Doniphan
b. 1787 - Fauquier County, Virginia

George Doniphan
b. 4 Jul 1790 - St. George's Parish, Fredericksburg, Virginia
d. 1864 - Augusta, Bracken County, Kentucky

Margaret Doniphan
b. 1792 - St. George's Parish, Fredericksburg, Virginia

Susan M. Doniphan
b. 12 Nov 1794 - St. George's Parish, Fredericksburg, Virginia

Lucy Doniphan
b. 1796 - St. George's Parish, Fredericksburg, Virginia

Matilda Doniphan
b. 1804 - St. George's Parish, Fredericksburg, Virginia
d. 1855 (Age 51 years)

Alexander William Doniphan
b. 8 Jul 1808 - Mason County, Kentucky
d. 8 Aug 1887 - Richmond, Ray County, Missouri

Ancestry

Joseph Doniphan was the son of Alexander Doniphan (before 1720–1768) and Mary (Waugh) Doniphan (1721–1783), both of Overwharton Parish, Stafford County, Virginia. Joseph served in the Continental Army during the American Revolution from Chadds Ford, Delaware County, Pennsylvania.[2] In 1779, "he went to Kentucky and taught school at [Boonesborough]" in Madison County. Returning to Virginia, he married Miss Smith on April 25, 1784 in Fauquier County. The couple and their young family migrated to Mason County, Kentucky, in 1791.[3]

The Doniphan's "descend from a Spaniard who was knighted by Phillip the Second for gallantry in the Moorish wars." Don Alphonso Iphan, "which was reduced and anglicized to Doniphan. The son of the Spanish ancestor married a Scotch heiress, Margaret Mott, and settled in the northern neck of Virginia in about 1650."[4]

Joseph and U.S. Supreme Court Justice Marshall were schoolmates in Virginia.[5] Joseph became a prosperous farmer and served as county sheriff.[6] Judge R. Kenneth Elliott (ret.) recorded that Alexander W. Doniphan's father had "been a teacher and friend of Daniel Boone."[7]

Alexander W. Doniphan's mother was a daughter of Captain Thomas Smith, a captain in the Virginia Light Horse.[8] Her brother was Colonel Walter Smith, and she was the "aunt of the celebrated Captain 'Extra Billy' Smith, who was elected Governor of Virginia in 1845, and served several times in Congress."

Childhood

On March 12, 1814, Alexander W. Doniphan's father, Joseph Doniphan, died unexpectedly at Clarks Run, Mason County, Kentucky, leaving his wife and several young children at home.[9] Alexander W. Doniphan, age five, was sent to live with his eldest brother, George Doniphan, in Augusta, Bracken County, Kentucky.[10] Eighteen years separated Alexander W. Doniphan with his eldest brother.[11] George Doniphan (1790- 1864) and family are all buried in the Augusta Hillside Cemetery in Augusta, Bracken County, Kentucky.[12]

Alexander W. Doniphan graduated "with high honors in his 19th year"[13] in 1826 from Bracken College at Augusta, Kentucky, and immediately began studying law under a prominent local attorney, Martin Marshall, "a kinsman of the first Chief Justice of the U.S. Supreme Court."[14] After three years of apprenticeship, Alexander W. Doniphan received in 1829 permission to practice law in Ohio and Kentucky.[15]

To Lexington, Missouri

The following year in 1830, Alexander W. Doniphan, at age twenty-two, emigrated up the Mississippi and Missouri Rivers, stopping and settling at Lexington, Lafayette County, Missouri. He gained admission to the Missouri Bar, and on April 19, 1830, "opened a law office" where he began a lengthy career as a defense attorney. Alexander W. Doniphan quickly became prominent on the Missouri frontier.[16] Judge Elliott stated Alexander W. Doniphan, "was a mighty orator with a commanding presence and persuasive manner."[17]

Give Us Liberty

In 1833, Alexander W. Doniphan moved to Liberty in Clay County, Missouri, which he regarded as home for the rest of his life.

Immediately, Alexander W. Doniphan became embroiled in a western border conflict that became known as the Mormon War, when local and Missouri state government and "settlers" turned on Mormon "Saints," to force them out of the state. Judge Elliott summed it up:

Doniphan was commander of a local militia unit and was credited for saving the life of Joseph Smith who was the leader of the Latter Day Saints Church (Mormons) at Far West, when he informed the General who had been ordered by the Missouri Governor to exterminate the Mormons, that if the General did kill these Mormons, Doniphan promised the General that he would see that the General would be prosecuted in the Courts for murder. The General decided not to exterminate the Mormons. Doniphan represented the Mormons in Court proceedings and in other matters when they were in Missouri.[18]

Alexander W. Doniphan and his fellow attorneys (David Rice Atchison, William T. Wood, and Amos Rees), however, were unsuccessful in their legal efforts on behalf of their Mormon clients.[19]

Alexander W. Doniphan continued his legal practice, and became a prominent, highly respected member of the community. Politically, Alexander W. Doniphan "was an admirer and supporter of Henry Clay."[20]

Alexander W. Doniphan was successfully elected to office. "His election to the Missouri General Assembly as Whig representative from Clay County in 1836 suggests the esteem in which his neighbors held him."[21] He was reelected in 1840 and 1854.[22] While in the state legislature, Alexander W. Doniphan was a colleague of Colonel John Thornton.[23]

Double Marriage

On December 21, 1837, Alexander W. Doniphan, age twenty-nine, married Thornton's seventeen-year-old daughter, Miss Elizabeth Jane

Thornton. She was born December 21, 1820, in Clay County, Missouri, to Colonel John and Mrs. Elizabeth (Trigg) Thornton. She was "one of the first children born in [Clay] County, when Missouri was a Territory."[24]

The marriage at the Thornton's Liberty home on this auspicious day was not only on Miss Thornton's birthday; but it was also a double-wedding ceremony. Elizabeth's sister, Caroline, also wed the same day to Oliver P. Moss.[25]

Pioneering Family

The Doniphans had two sons. The first, John Thornton Doniphan, named in honor of his paternal grandfather, was born on September 18, 1838. Alexander W. Doniphan's young family was enumerated in the 1840 U.S. Census. Alexander W. Doniphan in 1840 owned three African American slaves.

> Some twenty years before, Alexander W. Doniphan's brother, Thomas Smith Doniphan and wife, Rebecca (Frazee) Doniphan, moved from Kentucky in 1818 to Brown County, Ohio, "in order that he might set free the slaves in his employ.[26] Each person[27] who had called him 'Master' was given to understand that he was henceforth to be a free man, and for each a cabin was erected, in addition to the presentation of a horse and $50 in cash."[28]

The Doniphans' second son carried on his father's name, Alexander William, Jr., who was born on September 10, 1840. Sadly, both sons would perish before growing to adulthood.

WHITE MALES	WHITE FEMALES	SLAVE MALES	SLAVE FEMALES
1-under age 5	1, 15-19	1-under 10	1-under 10
1, 30-39			1, 10-23

Santa Fe Trail

The Santa Fe Trail had been a successful venture between Missouri and Santa Fe in Mexico since 1821, when Mexico gained its independence. However, bureaucratic governmental interference and corruption twenty years later was threatening the international thoroughfare. Harassment, occasional imprisonment of U.S. traders, and a brief Mexican embargo in 1843 increased American resentment of Mexican nationals.

Mexican War

Carl Beamer's dissertation on Doniphan's leadership in the Mexican War explains the American motivation for conflict. "By 1846, the Americans had become vocal in their desire either to annex New Mexico, or to force the Mexican government to change its policies, and thus remove these barriers to their prosperity. Therefore, they supported a war with Mexico. The annexation of Texas and attempts to acquire New Mexico and California were major causes of the Mexican War. Also, the Americans saw Chihuahua as the terminus of the Santa Fe trade. Because of its reported wealth and economic importance, many merchants traded there instead of at Santa Fe. To undertake the Santa Fe/Chihuahua campaign, the U.S. government called for volunteers from the various states and instructed General Stephen [Watts] Kearney, whom it had appointed to command the column aimed at Santa Fe, to integrate those from Missouri into his force."[29]

As the westernmost state, Missouri's citizens would be asked to serve. "Governor John C. Edwards, of Missouri, called for volunteers to join the 'Army of the West,'"[30] formed into companies under General Kearney at Fort Leavenworth. "The units that would follow Doniphan into Mexico included nine companies of mounted riflemen and an artillery battery. In addition, the Missourians also produced two infantry companies and another battery. Eight of the horse companies made up a regiment called the First Regiment, Missouri Mounted Volunteers: Company A from Jackson County under Captain David Waldo (116 men).

Company B from Lafayette County under Captain William Walton (112 men); Company C from Clay County under Captain O.P. Moss (119 men) [, etc.]…The total shows that Missouri contributed 1,388 men plus staff officers and company commanders to the initial invasion force."[31] They reached Santa Fe on August 18, 1846.[32]

Few of the campaigns of the Mexican War "are as remarkable as Colonel Alexander Doniphan's expedition into Chihuahua during the winter of 1846 to 1847. With approximately one thousand men, he invaded the major province of Northern

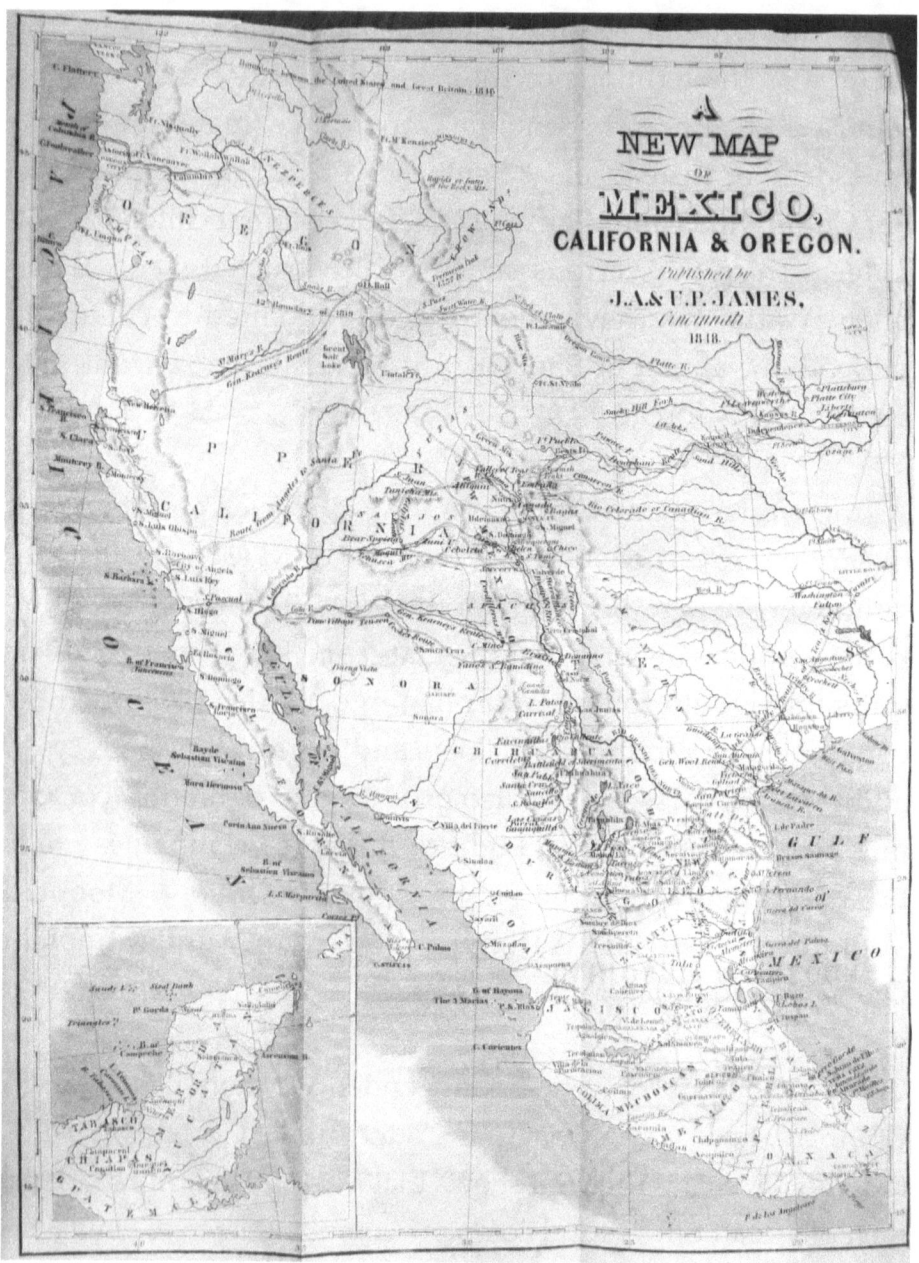

Mexico, fought and won two battles against larger Mexican forces and held the provincial capital until ordered to return."33

After the two battles, Alexander W. Doniphan never faced any serious danger from enemy forces and had little difficulty holding the

From the St. Louis New Era.
COL. DONIPHAN.

This commander has conducted his expedition with a degree of boldness and military skill that would not discredit a veteran in the service.

After crossing the extensive plains to Santa Fe, he was successfully engaged in reducing the Navajo Indians; then, with imperfect means of transportation and supply, he pushed forward to Chihuahua; met the enemy at Bracito, routing a superior force; took possession of El Paso, and advanced to attack the capital of the State. The conquest of Chihuahua was supposed to be a task which would require the united exertions of Wool and Doniphan, but has been affected by the latter alone, against tremendous odds, and with a full knowledge that the expected assistance to be derived from Wool would fail him. The victory was not only decisive, but will be attended with many salutary effects. It has brought relief and protection to American traders, whose property and lives were in jeopardy; has probably opened the way to new commerce with Chihuahua; has given fresh courage to our troops in Northern Mexico, and struck fresh terror to the bosoms of the enemy in that quarter.

The officers and men—all Missourians—have conducted themselves in a way which has done honor to themselves and to the State which sent them out. Missouri has some reason for pride and exultation.

To travel a thousand miles, then carry on a successful campaign against the Indian tribes, and afterwards to push forward seven hundred miles further—all in 6 months—would be deemed good work, even if a hostile Mexican had never shown himself to our forces. How much more, then, when their progress was resisted by forces four times their number, and operating in the heart of the enemy's own country.

All the movements and results of this fortunate campaign have, however, failed of saving Col. Doniphan from censure. In the outset he was charged with lack of energy, and injurious indulgence to the men under his command. But since his successful march and complete triumph through Chihuahua have shown the groundlessness of these charges, he has been assailed for his imprudence and rashness in venturing so far.

The reply to all this—overwhelming defeat for the enemy, and the great and, so far as concerns our forces, the almost bloodless possession of a large and populous State.

We trust that prejudice and envy had no share in originating these charges; but, from whatever source they come, we doubt not that the people of Missouri will take them at their true value, and treat them with the indifference which they so well deserve.

PROCLAMATION.
By the Commander-in-chief of the North American forces in Chihuahua.

The commander of the North American forces in Chihuahua, informs the citizens of this State, that he has taken military possession of this capitol, and has the satisfaction to assure them that complete tranquility exists therein.

He invites all the citizens to return to their houses, and continue their ordinary occupations, under the security that their persons, religion and property shall be respected.

He declares, likewise, in the name of his government, that having taken possession of the capitol, after conquering the forces of the State, he has equally taken possession of the State.

He invites the citizens of all the towns and *ranchors* to continue their traffic, to come to this capitol to buy and sell as formerly before the late occurrences, under the assurance they shall in no manner be molested or troubled, and as already said, their property shall be respected; for if the troops under my command should stand in need of anything, a fair price shall be given for the value thereof with the utmost punctuality.

He likewise declares, that the American troops will punish with promptitude any excess that may be committed, whether it be by the barbarous Indians or by any other individual.

Lastly, we assue all good citizens, that we carry on war against the armies alone, and not against individual citizens who are unarmed.

We, therefore, only exact, not that any Mexican should assist us against his country, but that in the present war he remain neutral; for it cannot be expected, in a contrary event that we should respect the rights of those who take up arms against our lives.

ALEXANDER W. DONIPHAN.
Commander-in-chief

The Liberty Tribune for May 22, 1847 included two installments regarding Doniphan.

Doniphan's Mexican War Expedition				
Date	Engagement	US Force		US Casualties
		Mexican Force		Mexican Casualties
25 Dec 1846	Battle of El Brazito, or "Little Arm" of the Rio del Norte	800		0 KIA; 8 wounded
		1,100		61 KIA;[34] 8 wounded; 150 POW
28 Feb 1847	Pass of the Sacramento	924		1 KIA;[35] 11 wounded
		4,000		304 KIA; 500 wounded; 40 POW

city of Chihuahua, thanks to the great desolate distances which separated him from organized Mexican opposition. "None of the other campaigns—Zachary Taylor's, Winfield Scott's, or John C. Fremont's—accomplished as much with such a small force or with as little difficulty."[36]

Beamer sums up Doniphan's service in the following way. "The success of Doniphan's campaign resulted in great part from his personal character and ability. His background had equipped him with the knowledge to understand and handle the independent Missourians."[37]

Super Jewel

Judge Elliott wrote that "after returning from the War, Doniphan became the first Superintendent of Schools and gave a commencement speech at the Academy at West Point.

"In 1849, Doniphan and others from Clay County, Missouri managed

Missouri Legislature granted a charter to found William Jewell College in Liberty, Missouri, in 1849.

to secure the establishment of a new college in Liberty, named William Jewell College, begun by the Baptists in Missouri. The college is a thriving institution to this day, attended by approximately 1600 students."[38]

Lawyer

Doniphan established a reputation as a successful lawyer in a frontier area where a man's character determined his position among his neighbors. His eloquent speech and debating ability had a greater effect on his achievements, however. "One early example of Doniphan's legal ability was his defense of Orrin Rockwell, a Mormon charged with conspiring to murder the Governor. Although the plot failed, public outrage coupled with strong anti-Mormon sentiments (due to Mormon religious beliefs) created a desire for revenge among the people against the defendant. In this case, Doniphan proved that he could sway

The image above is a section of the 1850 Census for Clay County, Missouri. Alexander Doniphan's mother is listed as Elizabeth Jane (Thorton) and his siblings, are enumerated in the adjoining household. The Slave Schedules did not appear to list Doniphan as a slaveholder in 1850.

public opinion, if not completely, at least to a great extent, a talent which would prove valuable when he attempted to command a group of independent citizen soldiers who objected to formal control. In the trial, even his eloquent arguments failed to overcome the anti-Mormon sentiment and the jury found Rockwell guilty. However, his abilities as a defense lawyer may never have shone brighter, for he was able to win a sentence of only five minutes in jail for his client."[39]

Trials of a Different Kind

The next five years would be filled with loss for the Doniphans. Their sons "were the pride of [their lives], and prospectively the prop and solace of their parents, as they encountered the decrepitude of advancing years. Unhappily, however, both of them, while youths, were killed accidentally."[40]

On May 9, 1853, their eldest son, John Thornton Doniphan, at age fourteen "died from accidental poisoning. While visiting his uncle James Baldwin, he sought relief for a toothache in the middle of the night but mistakenly took corrosive sublimate (mercury chloride), thinking that it was Epsom salts." His grief-stricken mother suffered a stroke at the burial, which left her a semi-invalid for the remainder of her life" as reported in *The Liberty Tribune*.

Then, five years later, Alexander William, Jr., a student at Bethany College in Bethany, Virginia (now, West Virginia), died tragically on May 11, 1858. "He drowned in a flood- swollen" Buffalo Creek in Wayne County. His body was returned to Liberty, Missouri, for interment in the family plot at Fairview Cemetery.[41]

The next twenty years, while filled with rewarding work for

DEATHS.

OBITUARY.

—In this county, on the 9th inst., at the residence of his uncle, James H. Baldwin, died JOHN THORNTON DONIPHAN, son of Alexander W. Doniphan, in the 14th year of his age.

The following are briefly the circumstances attending this melancholy event. On the night of the 3d inst., feeling somewhat indisposed, he awoke an affectionate Aunt who lay adjoining, who arose and, going to her drawer, took from it, as she supposed, a dose of Salts, which she had previously prepared for herself, but which proved to be, alas! *corrosive sublimate*, which had been placed in the drawer for safe keeping, as is supposed by a servant, but unfortunately without her knowledge.— This deadly poison, thus innocently given, was at once swallowed, when the fatal accident soon became evident. The most skillful medical aid was immediately called in, and the most assidious attention rendered, but all to no effect. Stealthily thus death had made his approach, and no skill could heal the wound which he had caused the hand of kindness to inflict. He bore away his victim, a noble boy, from the side of an only brother, while the fondest of parents bent over his pillow and besought their child to stay in vain.

We remember that fine brow, turned for many a classic honor, and that independent, careless air, that eye and manly port. Now is it so, that we shall no more strike our hand in thine and greet thee, Thornt, and hear thy modest parley? Is it so? Thornton thou art gone—

"Farewell! we yield thee to the tomb, with many a bitter tear,
Tho' 'twas not meet a soul like thine should longer tarry here—
Fond clustering hopes have sunk with thee that earth can ne'er restore;
Love casts a garland on thy turf that may not blossom more;
But thou art where each dream of hope shall in fruition fade
And love, immortal and refined, glow on without a shade."

The Liberty Tribune, May 13, 1853, obituary of John Thornton Doniphan

Alexander W. Doniphan, were shadowed with grief and sadness over the loss of his two sons. And, Alexander W. Doniphan would endure the forthcoming Civil War away from his hometown, all the while caring from his invalid wife into old age.

1860 Census

Mr. and Mrs. Doniphan, age fifty-one and thirty-nine respectively, were at home in Liberty, Missouri, when the U.S. Census enumerator came to their door in 1860. Separate Slave Schedules also listed them owning five African American slaves, to wit:

26-year-old black male	b. ca. 1834
25-year-old black male	b. ca. 1835
18-year-old black male	b. ca. 1842
18-year-old mulatto female	b. ca. 1842
12-year-old mulatto male	b. ca. 1848

Although a slave owner, Alexander W. Doniphan rejected Southern secession and favored the preservation of the Union.[42]

Civil War

Judge Elliott remarked, "At the advent of the Civil War, Doniphan went to Washington, D.C. as a member of the Peace

Conference in an attempt to avoid the Civil War, without success. It was on this occasion that Doniphan met Lincoln and they were asked to back up to one another to see who was the tallest, and their heights were the same."[43]

"When introduced to President Lincoln, the President said: 'And this is the Colonel Doniphan, who made the wild march against the Comanches and Mexicans. You are the only man I ever met whose appearance came up to my prior expectations."[44]

"Doniphan supported the U.S. government throughout his life and believed in obeying its dictates, even when these feelings ran counter to local sentiment during the Civil War."[45] To this end, Alexander W. Doniphan "served as a delegate to the failed Washington Peace Convention and was a participant at the 1861 Missouri Constitutional Convention, where he declared he was 'a Union man. I go for the whole Union, the entire Union. I go for it North, South, East, and West. I do not intend to bring about a calamity that will destroy the Border Slave States and the whole Union.' Governor Claiborne Fox Jackson offered Doniphan a commission in the Missouri State Guard, but Doniphan turned it down."[46]

"In 1863, Doniphan moved from Liberty to St. Louis. Since he was a strong Unionist and many of his friends and clients were Southern Sympathizers, he could not resolve the conflicts within himself, he lived in St. Louis during that period."[47]

1870 Census

After the war was over, the Doniphans moved to Richmond, Ray County, Missouri, where they were enumerated in the U.S. Census in 1870. They were aged sixty-one and forty-nine respectively. Mrs. Doniphan's eighty-two-year-old father, William Thornton, was living with them.

Five years after The Emancipation Proclamation, former slaves were enumerated with names as individuals in the U.S. Census for the first time.

There are only five black people in the U.S. who identified with the Doniphan surname in 1870. All were in one family unit living in Delaware, Leavenworth County, Kansas. Since the gender and ages do not match up with the slaves owned by Alexander W. Doniphan in 1860, they were not likely his former slaves. However, there were other Doniphan cousins (in St. Joseph, for instance) who may be connected:

    Louisa Doniphan; age 33; b. 1837 in Missouri
    Elizabeth   16   b. 1854 Missouri
    Mitchell   9   b. 1861 Missouri
    John   8   b. 1862 Missouri
    William   2   b. 1868 Kansas[48]

Four Score

Alexander W. Doniphan continued to practice law and established the Ray County Savings Bank.

Mrs. Elizabeth Doniphan died of a pulmonary hemorrhage on July 19, 1873 while on a trip to New York City.[49] His wife's death "threw a dark shadow across [Alexander W. Doniphan's] pathway to the end of his life. He never again married."[50] Fourteen years later, at the age of eighty, Alexander W. Doniphan died August 8, 1887, in Richmond, Ray County, Missouri. The Doniphans are buried in Fairview Cemetery, Liberty, Clay County, Missouri.[51]

Doniphan is remembered for his devotion to the rule of law, his belief in fairness, and his influential military and political service.[52] On the Courthouse grounds in Richmond, a life-sized statue of Doniphan by sculpted by fellow Missourian Frederick C. Hibbard was erected in 1918, and still stands more than 100 years later in 2019.[53]

Endnotes

1. https://www.colonial-settlers-md-va.us/getperson. php? personID = I024716&tree =Tree1 (viewed 25 June 2019). Other sources repeatedly say that Doniphan was the youngest of ten (10) children.

2. "Joseph Doniphan, although very young, joined the Colonial Army and served as a soldier during the entire Revolutionary struggle." Conard, Howard Lewis. Encyclopedia of the History of Missouri: A Compendium of History and Biography for Ready Reference. Volume 2. (Southern History Company, Haldeman, Conard & Company, proprietors, 1901), 292, as posted at http://goo.gl/Fygt5 (viewed 26 June 2019). "Joseph was with one or two of his brothers in the battle of Brandywine, his company being commanded by Capt. John Marshall. In this engagement an older brother, George Doniphan, was killed near him." https://www.adkins.ws/individual.php?pid=I3785 (viewed 26 June 2019).

3. Conard, 292, 295.

4. Conard, 295.

5. Conard, 295.

6. https://www.adkins.ws/individual.php?pid=I3785 (viewed 25 June 2019). Also, a letter from Alexander W. Doniphan to his cousin, Emma Doniphan, 22 Feb 1878, about his final trip to Kentucky and visiting his parents' graves on the farm where they had lived on Clarks Run. "Found the graves of my loved and revered parents in excellent repair, having been walled in with a heavy stone fence." From: dickpoll@aol.com http://archiver.rootsweb.ancestry.com/th/read/KYMASON/2004-05/1085314760

7. Elliott, R. Kenneth (Judge, retired). Alexander William Doniphan (1808–1887): https://www.claycountyarchives.org/j3x/index.php/resources/historical-info/58-alexander-william-doniphan (viewed 24 June 2019). Also, https://www.familysearch.org/service/records/storage/das-mem/patron/v2/TH-300-46686-38- 56/dist.txt?ctx=ArtCtxPublic (viewed 25 June 2019). This genealogy is contrary to undocumented and suspect genealogy of the Doniphan family on the Harry S. Truman Presidential Library and Museum website: https://www.trumanlibrary.org/genealogy/index.php?m=family&id=601 (viewed 24 June 2019).

8. Conard, 295.

9. Repetitive sources claim Alexander W. Doniphan's father died in 1813. https://www.adkins.ws/individual.php?pid=I3785 (viewed 26 June 2019). Conard, 292, adds that among the seven children was Alexander W. Doniphan's "older brother, Dr. Thomas S. Doniphan, who served as a surgeon during the War of 1812, and is the father of Colonel John Doniphan, a distinguished lawyer and excellent citizen of St. Joseph, [Buchanan County], Missouri."

10. Harper, Kimberly, text and research on Alexander W. Doniphan (1808-1887) posted at: https://shsmo.org/historicmissourians/name/d/doniphan/ (viewed 24 June 2019).

11. Launius, Roger D. Alexander William Doniphan: Portrait of a Missouri Moderate. (Columbia: University of Missouri Press, 1997), 2. Also, https://www.colonial-settlers-md-va.us/getperson.php?personID=I024716&tree=Tree1 (viewed 25 June 2019).

12. https://www.findagrave.com/memorial/63249551/george-doniphan (viewed 24 June 2019).

13. Conard, 292

14. Beamer, Carl. Effective Amateur: Alexander Doniphan's Leadership in The Mexican War 1846-1847. Thesis. Kansas State University, Manhattan, Kansas 1979, 3, as posted online at:https://krex.k-state.edu/dspace/bitstream/handle/2097/27010/LD2668T41979B42.pdf?sequence=1&isAllowed=y. Also, Elliott.

15. Beamer, 1.

16. Conard, 292.

17. Elliott.

18. Elliott. Also, Harper: "After trouble erupted once more between Mormons and non-Mormons, Missouri Governor Lilburn Boggs called upon the Missouri State Militia to intervene. Doniphan, a brigadier general in the militia, helped negotiate the surrender of Mormon leader Joseph Smith, Jr. and several other members of the group. General Samuel Lucas convened a military court martial and found Smith and his followers guilty of treason. Lucas then ordered Doniphan to execute the men by firing squad. As a firm believer in the rule of law, Doniphan held that the court martial was illegal because Joseph Smith and his men were civilians and that not all members of the court martial were members of the military. He refused to carry out General Lucas's command. Doniphan wrote Lucas, 'It is cold-blooded murder. I will not obey your order. My brigade shall march for Liberty tomorrow morning, at 8 o'clock; and if you execute these men, I will hold you responsible before an earthly tribunal, so help me God.' Lucas then placed Joseph Smith and his followers on trial at Richmond, Missouri. Doniphan once again served as the Mormon's legal counsel. While the men were being transferred on a change of venue to Columbia, all but two of them escaped and left the state. The two remaining men were acquitted."

19. Harper.

20. Elliott.

21. Beamer, 5.

22. Harper. Also, Conard, 293.

23. https://en.wikipedia.org/wiki/Alexander_William_Doniphan (viewed 24 June 2019).

24. https://www.findagrave.com/memorial/51253684/elizabeth-jane-doniphanquoting

Mrs. Doniphan's obituary in The Wakenda Record, 25 Jul 1873 (viewed 24 June 2019). The Thorntons's are also buried in Fairview Cemetery, Liberty, Clay County, Missouri https://www.findagrave.com/memorial/12004/john-thornton (viewed 24 June 2019).

25. https://en.wikipedia.org/wiki/Alexander_William_Doniphan (viewed 24 June 2019).

26. Originally written as "negroes."

27. Originally written as each colored person.

28. Conard, 296.

29. Beamer, 12-19.

30. Conard, 293.

31. Beamer, 21.

32. Conard, 293.

33. Beamer, 1.

34. Among those killed in action was General Ponce de Leon, who had been named for the Spanish explorer who years before "discovered" what became the state of Florida at St. Augustine.

35. Prominent Independence, Jackson County, Missouri, merchant, Major Samuel Combs Owens was killed at the Battle of Sacramento near Chihuahua, Mexico, and was buried there. https://www.findagrave.com/memorial/105096257/samuel-combs-owens (viewed

24 June 2019). Owens "voluntarily and with courage amounting to rashness, charged upon a redoubt and received a cannon or rifle shot which instantly killed both him and his horse." Conard, 294.

36. Beamer, 1.

37. Beamer, 3.

38. Elliott.

39. Beamer, 4.

40. Conard, 293.

41. https://en.wikipedia.org/wiki/Alexander_William_Doniphan (viewed 24 June 2019).

42. Harper.

43. Elliott.

44. Conard, 293.

45. Beamer, 4–5.

46. Harper.

47. Elliott.

48. This "may" be Thomas W. Doniphan (1867-1955) who is buried in Highland Cemetery, and African-American cemetery in Kansas City, Jackson County, Missouri. He married laundress Nettie (Johnson) Doniphan (1872–1956), daughter of William and Mary Johnson. Thomas and Nettie were the parents of Earnest Doniphan (1904–1920), and grandparents of Joseph Douglas Doniphan (1913–1950), all buried in Highland Cemetery. https://www.findagrave.com/memorial/137173059/thomas-w-doniphan (viewed 24 June 2019).

49. https://en.wikipedia.org/wiki/Alexander_William_Doniphan (viewed 24 June 2019).

50. Conard, 293.

51. Block 95, Lot 14 or 15, Spaces 2 and 3, as identified on their findagrave.com memorials.

52. Harper.

53. Elliott. Also, Harper.

Bibliography

Monographs and Serials

"Alexander William Doniphan: Symbol of Pioneer Americanism." *Liberty Advance*, 26 May 1947, 5.

American Heritage Pictorial Atlas of United States History. (New York: American Heritage Publishing Co., Inc., 1966).

Beamer, Carl. *Effective Amateur: Alexander Doniphan's Leadership in The Mexican War 1846-1847*. Thesis. Kansas State University, Manhattan, Kansas 1979; as posted online at: https://krex.k-state.edu/dspace/bitstream/handle/2097/27010/LD2668T41979B42.pdf?sequence=1&isAllowed=y.

Christensen, Lawrence O., William E. Foley, Gary R. Kremer, and Kenneth H. Winn, eds. *Dictionary of Missouri Biography*. (Columbia: University of Missouri Press, 1999), 246–47.

Clark, Kimball. "The Epic March of Doniphan's Missourians." *Missouri Historical Review* (January 1986) 80:2, 134–55.

"Colonel A. W. Doniphan Appointed Commissioner to Peace Convention at Washington." *Columbia Statesman,* 9 Feb 1861, 2:7, 3:1.

"Colonel Doniphan Refused Appointment under the New Military Bill." *Columbia Missouri Statesman,* 7 June 7 1861, 2:1.

"Colonel Doniphan Seriously Injured in Stagecoach Accident at Georgetown." Columbia Missouri Statesman, 29 Dec 1854, 2:3-4.

Conard, Howard Lewis. *Encyclopedia of the History of Missouri: A Compendium of History and Biography for Ready Reference*. Volume 2. (Southern History Company, Haldeman, Conard & Company, proprietors, 1901). Online Google Book @ http://goo.gl/Fygt5.

Culmer, Frederic A. "A Snapshot of Alexander W. Doniphan, 1808–1897." *Missouri Historical Review* (October 1943) 38:1, 25–32.

Dawson III, Joseph G. *Doniphan's Epic March: The 1st Missouri Volunteers in the Mexican War*. (Lawrence: University Press of Kansas, 1999).

Hamele, Ottamar. *When Destiny Called: A Story of the Doniphan Expedition in the Mexican War*. (San Antonio, TX: Naylor Co., 1948).

Launius, Roger D. *Alexander William Doniphan: Portrait of a Missouri Moderate.* (Columbia: University of Missouri Press, 1997).

Liberty Tribune, 22 May 1847, "From the St. Louis New Era, Col. Doniphan"

Liberty Tribune 22 May 1847
"Proclamation by the Commander-in-Chief of the North American Expeditionary Forces at Chihuahua"

Liberty Tribune, 13 May 1853
Deaths: Obituary

McGroarty, William B., ed. "Letters from Alexander W. Doniphan." *Missouri Historical Review* (October 1929) 24:1, 26–39.

McGroarty, William B., ed. "William H. Richardson's Journal of Doniphan's Expedition, Part 1." *Missouri Historical Review* (January 1928) 22:2: 193–206.

McGroarty, William B., ed. "William H. Richardson's Journal of Doniphan's Expedition, Part 2." *Missouri Historical Review* (April 1928) 22:3, 331–60.

McGroarty, William B., ed. "William H. Richardson's Journal of Doniphan's Expedition, Part 3." *Missouri Historical Review* (July 1928) 22:4, 511–42.

Robinson, Jacob S. *A Journal of the Santa Fe Expedition under Colonel Doniphan.* (Princeton: *Princeton University Press,* 1932).

Williamson, Hugh P. "Colonel Alexander W. Doniphan: Soldier, Lawyer, and Statesman." *Journal of the Missouri Bar* (October 1952) 8:10, 180.

Online Resources

https://shsmo.org/historicmissourians/name/d/doniphan (Kimberly Harper on Alexander W. Doniphan)

https://www.colonial-settlers-md-va.us/getperson.php? personID = 1024716&tree = Tree1

https://www.adkins.ws/individual.php?pid=I3785

https://www.claycountyarchives.org/j3x/index.php/resources/historical-info/58-alexander- william-doniphan

https://www.familysearch.org/service/records/storage/das-mem/patron/v2/TH-300-46686-38- 56/dist.txt?ctx=ArtCtxPublic
https://www.trumanlibrary.org/genealogy/index.php?m=family&id=601

https://shsmo.org/historicmissourians/name/d/doniphan/

https://www.colonial-settlers-md-va.us/getperson.php?personID=1024716&tree=Tree1

https://www.findagrave.com/memorial/63249551/george-doniphan
https://en.wikipedia.org/wiki/Alexander_William_Doniphan

https://www.findagrave.com/memorial/51253684/elizabeth-jane-doniphan
https://www.findagrave.com/memorial/12004/john-thornton

Ancestry.com
    U.S. Federal Census Population Schedules, 1840, 1850, 1860, 1870
    U.S. Federal Census Slave Schedules, 1840, 1850, 1860

terminated or driven from the State if nece-

Head Quarters of the Militia
City of Jefferson Oct 27 1838

...the order of this morning to you
...you to raise 400 mounted men to
...men your division I have rece...
...Rees Esq of Ray & Willock to willi...
...My Aid information of the most
...character which entirely changes t...
...ings and place the Mormons in t...
...of open and armed defiance of the ...
...of having made war upon the p...
...State Your orders are therefore t...
...ration with all possible speed
...ust be treated as enemies and m...
...minated or driven from the Sta...
...for the public peace— Their outra...
...all description— If you can me...
...you are authorized to do so to a...
...may consider necessary I ha...
...orders to Majr Genl Willock of...
...raise 500 men and to ma...
...Northern part of Daviess an...
...Genl Doniphow of Clay wi...
...with 500 men to proceed
...the purpose of intercepting
...to the North E...
...to communicate with you by ex...
...Also communicate with them if you p...
...cessary Instead therefore of proceeding as
...directed to reinstate the citizens of Daw...
...you will proceed immediately
...to operate against the
...Ray has been

CHAPTER 4

Alexander W. Doniphan: In Defense of Mormons

Dr. Susan Easton Black
Emeritus Professor of Church History and Doctrine
Brigham Young University

A history of the life of Alexander W. Doniphan focusing on his defense and representation of Mormon defendants during the Missouri Mormon wars.

Chapter Page Image: Governor Lilburn Boggs order to expell (or "exterminate if necessary") the Latter-day Saints from Missouri -- *Missouri Secretary of State - IT. "The Missouri Mormon War." Missouri Secretary of State. Accessed August 10, 2020. https://www.sos.mo.gov/archives/resources/findingaids/miscMormonRecords/eo.*

"There are few men whose names have been identified with the history of our Church, with more pleasant feelings to its members than General Doniphan," remarked Elder George A. Smith. "During a long career of persecution, abuse, and oppression, characters occasionally present themselves like stars of the first magnitude in defence [sic] of right, who are willing, notwithstanding the unpopularity that may attach to it, to stand up and protest against mob violence, murder, abuse, or the destruction of property and constitutional rights."[1]

Such a man was Alexander William Doniphan—known to his friends as Will. Books have been written about his military prowess in the Mexican War.[2] A statue located near the Richmond courthouse and a plaque where his home once stood in Liberty remind today's citizens of his unconquerable spirit during the U.S. campaign against Mexico.[3] But in Mormon circles, it is not his military conquests that have caused generations of the faithful to speak of him in near legendary terms. To them, Alexander W. Doniphan was and will always be the man who defended the Mormons and their leaders from injustice in Missouri.

Whether he applauded his defending role from 1833 until his death in 1887 is unknown. Yet he was publically complimentary of Latter-day Saints and their leaders: "I have never met a group of men who had native intelligence and understanding and force of character that have ever quite equalled [sic] the group of men—leaders gathered about Joseph Smith."[4] Although it is apparent Doniphan thought highly of Mormons, it does not appear that he cultivated a personal relationship with their leaders. Letters exchanged between Doniphan and the Mormon hierarchy speak only of business matters. His autobiography does not mention his interest in the persecuted religionists.

Wanting to fill the gap Doniphan neglected and to give credence to the deeds that military historians have discounted, I present a Mormon's view of Alexander William Doniphan. Would Doniphan object to such a remembrance? I think not. "Fortune does not shower her favors on us very often, and a man should not turn his plate bottom upwards when it does happen, but should turn the right side up and catch all he can," was his favorite metaphor.[5] As a Mormon who believes Doniphan still merits the "turned up plate" and all the plaudits that it can hold, I present a brief account of one Mormon's view of a life that intertwined with the beleaguered Latter-day Saints of Missouri in a remarkable way.

Years of Preparation

Historians trace the beginning of the Doniphan clan in the U.S. to Mott Doniphan, an Irishman who settled in Prince George County, Virginia, in 1670.[6] Among his descendants was Joseph Doniphan, the father of Alexander.[7] Joseph, like his much celebrated son, had a military and patriotic bent. He was a rebel in the Revolutionary Army and fought valiantly against the perceived tyranny of Britain. After the war, his marriage in 1785 to Anne F. Smith, daughter of Captain William Smith of the Virginia Light Horse militia, seemed well-positioned and all agreed they were suited for each other.

The young, but surely aspiring couple, settled in Mason County, Kentucky, in 1790. There Joseph amassed a fortune as a gentleman farmer. His role as local sheriff in helping rid the genteel society of the undesirable was only occasional work, as illustrated by the civil records of 1813 which show that he owned a prosperous estate in the Ohio River town of Augusta and had eighteen slaves. Between his wealth, his toiling slaves, and happy marriage blessed with eight children, even skeptical neighbors agreed that fortune had smiled upon the Doniphan clan.

But it was their eighth child, Alexander William Doniphan, who became the personification of good fortune, long after his father was forgotten. Alexander was born on July 9, 1808 in Maysville, Mason County, Kentucky.[8] At an early age he seemed destined to follow the exemplary military career of his progenitors. But such destiny, as with most lives, would wait for fulfillment as unexpected events diverted his course.

The first, and surely the most excruciating event, was the death of his father when Alexander was a mere child of four years old. Knowing of his pending demise and wanting more for his last son than fleeting childhood memories, Joseph bequeathed to Alexander a slave named Stephen and nearly half of his farmland in Mason County.[9] Unknowingly, his generosity proved a detriment to young Alexander. Most nineteenth century Kentuckians believed schooling was the gateway to opportunity and land left to a boy, not yet of school age, in a backwoods community often hampered a child's advancement in scholastic attainment.

To assure young Alexander's future education, by age eight he was sent to live with his older brother George and his wife Mary Ann Marshall in Augusta, Bracken County, Kentucky, about fifteen miles from his home.[10] At that time, school masters in Augusta boasted that their ability to educate the young was unrivaled. Their prideful boasts proved true for Alexander, for by age fourteen he was prepared to matriculate into Augusta College. Four years later this Methodist Episcopal academy graduated Alexander with honors. Thus, by age eighteen he was recognized by society as educated and prepared to launch into frontier life as a gentleman farmer of his own estate.

But such was not to be. It wasn't land that beckoned to him, but the pomp and ceremony he found in the profession of law. Martin Marshall, father of his sister-in-law and brother of the great jurist John Marshall, chief justice of the U.S. Supreme Court, agreed to tutor him in the rudiments of the justice system. Doniphan believed, "His legal preceptor was one of the most learned and able of all the members of the famous Marshall family."[11] Therefore, it was with pleasure that for nearly three years he studied in his law office before successfully passing the state bars in Ohio and Kentucky in 1829, and in Missouri in March 1830.

With law credentials in-hand and in the spirit of a youthful adventurer, Alexander bid farewell to loved ones and his law tutor and moved on April 19, 1830 to the Missouri frontier. There he joined a wave of newcomers from Kentucky, Tennessee, and Virginia, who had brought with them sixty thousand slaves in the 1820s in hope of extending the southern lifestyle to the western outpost of the U.S. As these southern farmers settled near the trading post of Independence, Missouri, they contrasted with the rough fur traders and beaver trappers who passed through the community on their way to the Santa Fe Trail. The sites and sounds of the new South and the rugged frontier in western Missouri captivated Alexander. This was where he would begin life anew as Doniphan—the lawyer, statesmen, and citizen/soldier.

Doniphan first established himself as a community lawyer in Lexington, a city of nearly two thousand inhabitants. As with most hopefuls, his initial law practice failed. By 1833 he had moved to Liberty, Clay County, a small village of three hundred residents. There he joined Kentuckian, David Rice Atchison, in a law partnership. "[We] might have been more successful attorneys, had [we] stayed in [our] offices more and out of the woods or at parties or in political caucuses less," lamented Doniphan.[12] He could have added, but perhaps chose not to record, that if both partners had enjoyed card games and other forms of gambling, horse racing, and evenings sitting in taverns with friends less, their practice might have grown faster.

In spite of societal vises, Doniphan did make a legal difference in Liberty and eventually western Missouri. His partner said of him:

> I was familiar with the city of Washington in my early manhood. I knew all the great men of our country in the earlier days—Clay, Webster, Calhoun, John Quincy Adams...and others. I have presided in the United States Senate when Clay, Webster, and Calhoun sat before me. I knew Aleck Doniphan familiarly, intimately, since 1830, and I tell you, sir, when he was in his prime I heard him climb higher than any of them.[13]

Recognizing the legal ability of Doniphan, clients sought his counsel on such diverse issues as delayed shipments of hogs, land titles, legal rights to slaves, and criminal activities. None of the legal forays he accepted were as exciting to him as defending accused criminals. His defense of over 180 men and his arguments before the Missouri State Supreme Court still leave admirers convinced that most of the accused were acquitted or received a lighter sentence due to his legal ability.

To them, his courtroom demeanor had the marks of a debater more than the library persona of a scholar. He argued plausibly, but rarely with any depth. His plausible approach, interspersed with his flair for theatrics, insured him of a crowded courtroom. Spectators came to recognize that when the courtroom heated with angry debate, Doniphan would speak in a high-pitched tone and pull on his sleeves in what appeared to the unwary as a nervous twitch. The judge, seeking decorum in his court, would shout, "Order in the Courtroom!" Ignoring the heavy sound of the gavel and the judicial demand, Doniphan would pull his sleeves up higher, raise his voice louder, and really go to work.

His performance was so legendary that after one judge issued a verdict of "not guilty," Doniphan, not the freed man, was carried out of the courtroom on the shoulders of the crowd. It is no wonder that a contemporary characterized him as an "absolute master at the bar" and friend D.C. Allen said when he spoke, "even swarming blackbirds in the trees grew silent in appreciation."[14]

Unfortunately, his combative theatrical approach to justice caused him personal problems. Although he was an imposing man, standing 6 feet and 4 inches in height, or as one memorial eulogizes "of immense stature, noble appearance, brilliant parts, fearless, of great moral courage, sanguine, faithful, just, poetic in temperament, the champion of the down-trodden, eloquent beyond description," he suffered from delicate health.[15] His courtroom appearances too often aggravated his physical problems.

It was not unusual for Doniphan to fall ill after an emotion-laden defense. The illness, undefined by medical practitioners of his day, required bed rest for several weeks.

In spite of the malady that drained his energy and required complete quiet, Doniphan did not publicly lament his fate. His only stated public regret for his theatrical antics in the courtroom was, "having been the cause of so many scoundrels going unhung."[16] Only two texts of his courtroom arguments have been preserved in their entirety. Reading these texts, which are splattered with repetitive expletives, will not leave even ardent historians wanting to read more. In his case, more courtroom transcripts may detract from the mystic of our hero before we align him with the Mormons.

However, his unchecked speech pattern did not stop students from wanting to study law under his tutelage. He accepted only a handful of students, but none more famous than the Mormon Prophet Joseph Smith and his associate Sidney Rigdon. "Rigdon and myself commenced this day the study of law, under the instruction of Generals Atchison and Doniphan," wrote the Prophet. "They think, by diligent application, we can be admitted to the bar in twelve months." Of the two students, it was Rigdon that Doniphan heard argue a case. On January 25, 1839 in the circuit court at Liberty, Rigdon was his own defense attorney.[17] After listening to his poignant defense, Doniphan said, "Such a burst of eloquence it was never my fortune to listen to, at its close there was not a dry eye in the room, all were moved to tears."[18]

Doniphan Defends the Mormons

Tutoring the Mormon Prophet and his associate Rigdon was not the first experience Doniphan had with the oft-hated Mormons of Missouri. His association with members of The Church of Jesus Christ of Latter-day Saints began in 1831 in the trailhead community of Independence. Doniphan had gone to Independence in hopes of having a suit made in the latest Eastern style. His hopes were realized after hiring Peter Whitmer, a tailor by trade and one of the first Mormon missionaries to enter Missouri.

Two years passed before Doniphan's name was again associated with a Mormon. Events of those two years were tumultuous for early Latter-day Saint settlers in Jackson County, Missouri. Although they had come to the area hoping to establish a millennial society, by 1833 they had lost their property, their legal rights, and were residing as exiles in Liberty. These problems led them to approach four local attorneys, including Doniphan, seeking legal assistance for wrongs suffered in Jackson County. Doniphan, with the other attorneys, agreed to accept the Mormons as clients with the stipulation that $250 be paid in advance for their legal services. "We have been doing a [legal] practice here among these people, to a considerable extent, and by this engagement we must expect to lose the greatest part of it," Doniphan explained. He apologized that "the circumstances here involved make it necessary" to ask for the financial advancement.[19]

The advancement proved wise for when news of their hire reached Jackson County, Doniphan and his associates were threatened by mobocrats for accepting Mormons as their clients. Although threatened, on December 6, 1833 the attorneys drafted a resolution to Governor George Dunklin seeking military intervention on behalf of their Mormon clients. They arbitrated with Jackson County officials, but as their clients were unwilling to accept anything less than a return of their lands and compensation for losses, the attorneys were unable to negotiate a compromise. The result was defeat.

The judicial defeat angered Doniphan. When he learned that the Mormons had rallied a quasi-military force to right the wrongs that legal negotiations could not, he cheered their actions:

> They are better citizens than many of the old inhabitants. That's a fact, and as the Mormons have armed themselves [in what became known as Zion's Camp], if they don't fight, they are cowards. I love to hear that they have brethren coming to their assistance, greater love can no man show, than he, who lays down his life for his brethren.[20]

But the Mormons needed more than cheer. Their attempt to right the wrong through military might failed, and on its heels came demands from Clay County officials to leave the county or be forced out. The urgency of their situation was accentuated by a mass meeting held on June 29, 1836 in the Liberty Courthouse, in which it was resolved, "We, therefore, in the spirit of frank and friendly kindness do advise them to seek a home where they may obtain large and separate bodies of land, and have a community of their own." Furthermore, county officials proposed "that [Mormon] emigration cease, and cease immediately, as nothing else can or will allay for a moment, the deep excitement that is now unhappily agitating this community."[21]

Fearful of the growing hostility, Mormons turned to Doniphan for help. Doniphan knew of the need to diffuse the situation which was escalating toward war. He turned to the state legislature in hopes of reaching a peaceful resolution. This turn was not a leap of faith, but one of confidence. In 1836, Doniphan had won a two-year term to the House of Representatives in the Missouri General Assembly. Although a new member of the legislature, he had already established a reputation of not taking the popular stance. He had voted "nay," much to the consternation of his colleagues, to a resolution to tender to President Andrew Jackson "respect, esteem, and best wishes for his future happiness at his retirement."[22] So speaking on behalf of the hated Mormons would be just one more minority stance.

Without fear of retribution, Doniphan alerted the General Assembly of the situation in Clay County and advocated that a new county be created for the Mormons that extended 48 miles north from the boundary of Ray County. He took a strong stand in affirmation of his proposal and withstood heavy opposition from influential state representatives for a time. But the opposition swayed other legislators into accepting a compromise that created two counties instead of one. On December 23, 1836, a bill to organize the counties of Caldwell and Daviess passed the House, the Senate agreed on December 27, and Governor Lilburn W. Boggs signed the bill into law on December 29.[23]

Although the bill did not stipulate restrictions on which county the Mormons could settle, it was assumed that Caldwell County would be a reserve for them, similar to reserves or reservations for Native Americans.[24] "If the Mormons are willing to go into the prairie country and settle, let them have it," was the general response to the bill.[25] Doniphan's disappointment with the new law was conveyed to Mormon leader W.W. Phelps, "I did not succeed as you wished or as you might have expected, in fixing the boundaries of your county…I was forced to report a bill making two counties north of Ray, instead of one."[26] But his diplomacy did create a window of hope and a temporary solution to escalating persecution of the Mormons.

As Mormons from Clay County packed their meager belongings and moved into Caldwell County, surprisingly Doniphan became a passive bystander. A teenager, the oldest daughter of Colonel John Thornton, captured his attention.[27] Elizabeth Jane Thornton became his bride on December 21, 1837, the day she turned seventeen.[28] "I was glad she had no more education than the Common Schools of this frontier then afford[ed]; I desired to educate her myself," wrote Doniphan. "I never read a book to myself (other than a law work) during the more than thirty years of married life; I read them all to her and with her."[29] To him, she was as "a child, wife, parent, and a friend of the poor and humble, she discharged a Christian's duty."[30]

Enamored by his choice, Doniphan took his bride to his residence at 124 North Main Street in Liberty and there enjoyed her company and his new familial role.[31] As his relationship grew ever closer to his wife, it appeared to outsiders that Doniphan had taken an extended respite from public life and Mormon concerns. But such views were short-lived. He, like other men in his community, had enrolled in the Clay County militia under the command of Captain Oliver Perry Moss. Never anticipating that the militia unit would be called to active duty, Doniphan was satisfied with his subservient role as a private. But shortly after his marriage, community leaders encouraged him to seek an appointment as a brigadier general. Although it appears such a dramatic change in rank is most unusual, the prevailing belief in the 1830s was that the nation's defense was best entrusted to its ordinary citizens. In compliance with their encouragement, Doniphan sent a letter to Governor Boggs requesting a change in rank.

Before his first wedding anniversary, he learned that his military appointment had been granted and that he was to gather troops and enforce an extermination order against the Mormons. Although he did rally troops, in a report to the governor he penned, "I disregarded that part [extermination] of his order, as the age of extermination was over."[32] Nevertheless, for eleven days his troops were in the field attempting to discharge the governor's demands. Then in the late afternoon of November 1, 1838, citizen/soldier Doniphan distinguished himself as a loyal defender of Latter-day Saints. Although he was a subordinate to General John B. Clark and General Samuel D. Lucas, on that date Doniphan defied military rule in behalf of Mormon leaders.

At a court-marital held against Joseph Smith and other Mormon leaders, Doniphan informed those present that he would defend the prisoners for they "had never belonged to any lawful military organization and could not therefore have violated military law."[33] He decried the court martial as "illegal as hell."[34] But in spite of his plausible arguments and famed theatrics, the prisoners were condemned to death, and Doniphan was ordered to carry out the execution:

> Sir: You will take Joseph Smith and the other prisoners into the public square of Far West, and shoot them at 9 o'clock to-morrow [sic] morning.
>
>   Samuel D. Lucas
>   Major-General
>   Commanding[35]

He replied:

> It is cold-blooded murder. I will not obey your order. My brigade shall march for Liberty to-morrow [sic] morning, at 8 o'clock; and if you execute those men, I will hold you responsible before an earthly tribunal, so help me God!
>
>   A.W. Doniphan
>   Brigadier-General[36]

Privately, Doniphan told Lucas, "You hurt one of these men if you dare, and I will hold you personally responsible for it, and at some other time you and I will meet again when in mortal combat, and we will see who is the better man."[37] To Mormon prisoner Lyman Wight, he said:

> Wight, your case is a d—— hard one; you are all sentenced to be shot tomorrow morning at eight o"clock on the public square in Far West—I wash my hands against such cold-blooded and heartless murder. He also said he should move his troops, numbering three hundred, before sunrise the next morning and would not witness such hard-hearted, cruel, and base murder. He then shook hands with me and bade me farewell.[38]

Then true to his word, on the morning of November 2, 1838, Doniphan departed with his troops for Clay County.[39] He was mustered out at Liberty on November 5, 1838. His pay for the eleven days of active duty and that of his servant or slave was $67.35.[40]

Angered by the military court martial and anxious to right the wrongs suffered by Mormon prisoners, Doniphan and his new law partner, Amos Rees, stepped forward to defend Latter-day Saint leaders at a legal hearing in Richmond. Of their legal service Joseph Smith wrote, "We could get no others in time for the trial. They are able men and will no doubt do well."[41]

The civil hearing at Richmond, often referred to as a "mock trial," began on November 12, 1838 and ended on November 28. Austin A. King,[42] fifth judicial circuit court judge, presided; William T. Wood and Thomas C. Burch served as prosecuting attorneys, and Alexander W. Doniphan and Amos Rees[43] represented the prisoners.[44] Seated in the courthouse was a hostile audience. "Shoot your Mormon, I have shot mine," one man shouted. Another exclaimed, "That dam [sic] rascal was in the battle—or out to Davis—or to De-Wit, such a one is a great preacher and leader amongst them, he ought to be hung, or sent to the penitentiary."[45]

When the first day of the hearing ended, Governor Boggs was informed:

> We progress slowly, but thus far the disclosures indicate certain conviction of treason against Smith, Wight, Pratt, Rigdon and some one or two more; and of murder against some five or six; burglary against

several; arson against a number; and larceny against others. How it will all result, I cannot tell, but that the leaders will be convicted of treason or murder I think is reasonably certain and many others of felony. You shall be informed as we progress.[46]

On that same day, the Mormon Prophet wrote to his wife:

My Dear Emma,

…we are prisoners in chains, and under strong guards, for Christ sake and for no other cause…but on examination, I think that the authorities, will discover our innocence, and set us free…I am your husband and am in bands and tribulation & c--
Joseph Smith Jr.[47]

The remaining fifteen days of trial focused on alleged Mormon raiding expeditions in Daviess County, the Battle at Crooked River, and the suspected treason of Mormon leaders. The prosecution called forty-one witnesses sworn in at the point of a bayonet. The prisoners listened to a seemingly endless parade of perjured witnesses who sought to verify old rumors by creating new ones. After eliciting testimony about Joseph Smith's teachings regarding the prophecy in Daniel 7:27 of the kingdom of God rolling forth and destroying all earthly kingdoms, Judge King instructed the clerk, "Write that down; it is a strong point for treason."[48] Doniphan objected to the comment but was overruled. He retorted, "Judge, you had better make the Bible treason."[49]

Following the examination of the prosecution witnesses, the defense attempted to introduce witnesses on behalf of the prisoners.

The attempt was a mere charade of justice as potential witnesses were taken as prisoners. Doniphan said:

> It was a damned shame that these defendants should be treated in this manner—that they could not be permitted to get one witness before the court, whilst all their witnesses, even forty at a time, have been taken by force of arms and thrust into that damned "bull pen," in order to prevent them from giving their testimony.[50]

At the conclusion of the trial, the judge ordered six prisoners (Joseph Smith, Hyrum Smith, Sidney Rigdon, Lyman Wight, Caleb Baldwin, and Alexander McRae) to Liberty Jail on charges of "overt acts of treason." He then gaveled the preliminary hearing to a close. Exasperated by his ruling, Doniphan exclaimed, "If a cohort of angels were to come down, and declare we were innocent, it would all be the same; for he [King] had determined from the beginning to cast us into prison."[51]

Doniphan's legal fee for his defense was extraordinary for the time—$5,000. Lacking the requisite funds to pay his bill, on November 28, 1839 Mormon Edward Partridge and his wife, Lydia, stepped forward and executed a deed for 1,079.86 acres in Jackson County to pay Doniphan.[52] He accepted the acreage as payment even though Joseph Smith advised him—

> ...not to take that Jackson County land in payment of the debt. God's wrath hangs over Jackson County. God's people have been ruthlessly driven from it, and you will live to see the day when it will be visited by fire and sword. The Lord of Hosts will sweep it with the besom of destruction. The fields and farms and houses will

be destroyed, and only the chimneys will be left to make the desolation.[53]

Doniphan's Popularity Not Hampered

With more land in his name and fathering two sons—John Thornton Doniphan born September 18, 1838 and Alexander Doniphan, Jr., born September 10, 1840, western Missourians concurred that no ill wind followed Doniphan for his defense of the Mormons. They pointed to his popularity among local constituents, his applauded service on the Board of Trustees of the William Jewell College, and his election to a second term in the state legislature in 1840. His 1842 defense of Orrin Porter Rockwell, a feared Mormon guard charged with attempted murder of the former Governor Boggs brought only publicity, but not rancor to Doniphan. Rockwell had been arrested in St. Louis and taken by stagecoach to Independence, where he was incarcerated for nine months. Twice he was escorted from the Independence Jail to Liberty to stand trial and twice Doniphan defended him. The last time he succeeded in getting him released with a punishment of just five more minutes in jail. He then personally released Rockwell.

Truly, for Doniphan, his plate of good fortune was overflowing. But he was not satisfied. Acquisition of rentals and personal property became his passion.[54] He entered land and business partnerships from Clay County to the Platte River. He invested in such diverse business ventures as the Liberty Insurance Company and the Hamilton Ferry on the Platte River.

It seemed as if his financial reach in western Missouri knew no bounds until his receipt of a letter from Missouri Governor John C. Edwards. The official letter ordered Doniphan to raise volunteer recruits to fight in the Mexican War. Doniphan, like other citizen/soldiers, willingly left his fortune to answer the patriotic call. From 1846 to 1847, he fought in bloody invasions of Mexico. His stunning victories elevated him to an unusual group of men—American heroes. His name became associated with General Zachary Taylor, frontiersman Ben McCulloch, and pathfinder John C. Fremont. As philosopher Alexis de Tocqueville phrased it, the army of a democracy "allows extraordinary men to rise about the common level."[55] And Doniphan was one of those who reached beyond.[56]

Doniphan and his First Missouri Mounted Volunteer Regiment believed in America's Manifest Destiny and fought for it with their very lives. The regiment not only captured portions of the state of New Mexico in August 1846, but six months later diverted Mexican soldiers from Santa Ana's army at the Battle of Buena Vista. Victories against Mexican soldiers greater in number than his own did not go unnoticed. General Stephen W. Kearny, Commander of the Army of the West, ordered Doniphan to subjugate all of New Mexico, defeat hostile Native Americans,[57] and draft a constitution and code of laws for the conquered region.

While attempting to fulfill what an ordinary man would have deemed impossible, Doniphan, with a love for theatrics, welcomed the famed Mormon Battalion into Santa Fe with a 100-gun salute. He then walked among the men of the battalion searching for Mormon friends and was "pleased to find a number of old acquaintances and friends among the soldiers."[58]

After the war, Doniphan and his regiment returned to Missouri, where many festive celebrations were held in their honor. At a public dinner in Independence on July 29, 1847, ladies presented him with a laurel wreath, symbolic of his victories. He accepted the wreath and all invitations to speak and celebrate the military victories for one year. But tired of the public adulation, he delivered a final address:

> My old fellow-soldiers, we will never all meet again. The green sod grows above many of our loved and honored comrades, and we too, must soon obey the last call to duty. It is plain that men had a beginning. It is a more grave and startling truth that we can never have an ending. In despite of our wishes or acts, we must live forever. Everything of which man takes cognizance had a beginning and must have an ending, but himself. The sun with all its glory must grow dim; the heavens with all their grandeur must pass away; but man is destined to immortal youth, under a sun that will never set, and in a world that will never pass away. That we may all be prepared for this last solemn call and the enjoyment of a glorious hereafter is the sincere prayer of your old comrade.[59]

He returned to his law practice and his financial quests, but without the same passion. Yet again he was successful as evidenced by the 1850 Missouri Census, which lists him as possessing $10,000 in real wealth.[60] But his focus had turned to public welfare. His service on the United States Military Academy Board at West Point, as Commissioner of Common Schools for Clay County in 1854, and his membership in the Clay County Agricultural and Mechanical Association belied his new interest in the public domain.

His growing concern for the good of others and his continued popularity led officials of the Whig Party to extend an invitation to him to run for congress. He declined. In 1852, they approached him to run for governor of Missouri, but again he declined. Historians purport that his refusals were based on the death of his son, John Thornton Doniphan, who died at the home of his uncle on May 9, 1853 after mistaking poison for medicine.[61] Extended family members suggest that a stroke or severe depression that afflicted his wife after his son's death was the cause. Perhaps it was both, but for personal reasons, Doniphan refused to be in the state spotlight. However, in 1854 he did accept an invitation to represent Clay County for a third term in the legislature. But even this service faded when his only remaining son, Alexander Doniphan, Jr., drowned in a stream on May 11, 1858.[62] With his sons gone, boys he viewed as "the most highly e ducated" in the state, the statesman and military leader Doniphan could not be consoled.[63]

Personal Sorrows Did Not Deter His Defense

Although never religious before the personal loss, Doniphan and his wife joined the Liberty Christian Church.[64] For a few years they were devout members and entertained in their home religious leaders like Alexander Campbell. But this graceful period of their lives ended all too abruptly when secession became the watchcry of slave holders in Clay County. Although an owner of five slaves valued at more than $4,000 and President of the Clay County Pro-Slavery Aid Association, Doniphan countered their cries. He organized and presided over an anti-secession rally in Liberty. Printed handbills announcing the rally attracted hundreds, if not thousands, who wanted to hear his views. They shivered through a three-hour snowstorm to listen as Doniphan pled for loyalty to the Union.

His views were widely quoted and directly led to his appointment as a delegate to the Washington Peace Conference that opened on February 4, 1861 at the Willard's Hotel in Washington, D.C..[65] The gathering, often referred to as the "Old Gentlemen's Convention" called for a united nation.[66] Doniphan supported the conference compromise that extended the Missouri line to the Pacific and allowed slavery south of that line.[67] But he did not support the presidency of Abraham Lincoln, even though he met him at the conference. "And this is the Colonel Doniphan who made the wild march against the Comanches and Mexicans. You are the only man I ever met who, in appearance, came up to my previous expectation," said Lincoln upon being introduced to Doniphan.[68] Doniphan wrote of Lincoln to his nephew John on February 22, 1862:

> It is very humiliating for an American to know that the present and future destiny of his country is wholly in the hands of one man, and that such a man as Lincoln—a man of no intelligence, no enlargement of view and ridiculously vain and fantastic as a country boy with his first red morocco hat…Jesting aside, old Abe is simply an ignorant country buffoon who makes about as good stump speeches as Jim Craig.[69]

Doniphan left the peace conference with little hope of avoiding the impending war. When fighting broke out between the states, he refused to command the pro-Southern troops from Missouri citing personal and family reasons. In April 1862, he urged all those at Liberty caught in the web of the secession delusion to abandon that cause, lay down their arms, and take the oath of allegiance.[70] Few heeded his words.

These were difficult days for Doniphan. Morally, he believed that he could not fight against the country he had served. He also believed that he could not raise arms against his Southern friends. Caught in the middle, Doniphan chose to sit out the Civil War.[71] He practiced law in Liberty until late 1863, when he and his wife moved to St. Louis, presumably to get away from the border conflict. From 1863 to 1868, they resided in St. Louis. There Doniphan processed military cases of widows and children as a claims agent.

Then in 1868, Doniphan and Jane moved to Richmond, Ray County, where he practiced law until his retirement in 1875, and served as president of the Ray County Savings Bank. But most of his time was consumed with the care of his wife. She had been a near invalid since the deaths of their sons and required almost constant care. While being cared for by a sister in New York, she succumbed to death on July 19, 1873 at the age of fifty-one. Upon learning of her demise, Doniphan wrote, "Her loss was the misery of my life." It was the "agony of his heart."[72]

Believing that travel to a mild climate would improve his health, if not attitude, in May 1874, Doniphan ventured to the Rocky Mountains. On Friday, May 22, 1874, he arrived in Salt Lake City. There he stayed at the Townsend House and was treated with great kindness by the Latter-day Saints. After one week in Utah, he traveled to Denver, where he enjoyed health spas and luxury hotels.

After returning to Missouri in 1875, he wrote to his cousin Emma,

> I am now an old man, sixty-seven, and after an active and not eventful life—greatly varied with sunshine and shadow—I am now isolated and alone; like the tall oak whose graceful boughs and delicate foliage has been torn ruthlessly away by the bolt of heaven and the old trunk is left standing awaiting the sure process of decay and death...I am now boarding at a Hotel with no one of my family in the county. It is a great change but far better than to live in the family of another. You can make a hotel a sort of home by using money and being quiet and conciliatory—and the family are old acquaintances and very kind to me.[73]

Hoping that interacting with others would lift his morale, Doniphan walked the main square in Richmond each day looking for friends. Residents reported that it took him an hour to go one block, because so many admirers wanted to converse with him. Graciously, he granted interviews, wrote newspaper columns, and counseled Missouri political leaders.

Of all those Doniphan spoke with, none seemed more concerned than the former Mayor of Richmond, David Whitmer. He had been confronted with a rumor purporting that he had denied his testimony of the existence of gold plates from which Joseph Smith had translated the Book of Mormon. Wanting to curtail the rumor, Whitmer asked Doniphan and other leaders in Richmond to listen to his testimony. "[My] testimony as recorded in the Book of Mormon is absolutely true, just as it is written there."[74] He then asked them to sign an affidavit attesting to his character and moral integrity on March 19, 1881:

> We, the undersigned citizens of Richmond, Ray County, Mo., where David Whitmer, Sr., has resided since the year A.D. 1838, certify that we have been long and intimately acquainted with him, and know him to be a man of the highest integrity, and of undoubted truth and veracity.[75]

After his endorsement of Whitmer, other Mormons sought an audience with Doniphan. John Morgan and Matthias F. Cowley reported that on April 13, 1882, "During the day we called on Gen. A. W. Doniphan, and had quite a talk with him, visited the cemetery, and the spot where the jail stood in which Joseph and Hyrum were confined."[76] On June 29, 1884 Heman C. Smith and William H. Kelley reported:

> We called on General Doniphan, who received us kindly, and expressed himself as being glad to meet us. He said the Mormons lived neighbors to him while they were in Clay County, and they were a moral people…The General informed us that he had examined the original manuscript [of the Book of Mormon] and being acquainted with Oliver Cowdery's handwriting, was positive it was principally written by him.[77]

History recorded that Smith and Kelley were his last Mormon visitors. On Monday, August 8, 1887 Doniphan died from bronchitis and congestion in Richmond at age seventy-nine. Following his funeral, he was buried near the remains of his wife in the Fairview Cemetery at Liberty. Thus, ended the life of a man, whom faithful Mormons speak of as a defender—a man who respected the law enough to defend even Mormons from injustice.

Endnotes

1. George A. Smith, Address delivered at Salt Lake City, May 24, 1874, *Journal of Discourses*. Liverpool: Latter-day Saints' Book Depot, 1875, 17:91.

2. Doniphan's papers, including a manuscript autobiography, are in the Missouri Historical Society at St. Louis. For biographical sketches see Howard L. Conard, *Encyclopedia of the History of Missouri: A Compendium of History and Biography for Ready Reference*. New York: The Southern History Company, 1901, and W. L. Webb, *Battles and Biographies of Missourians*. Kansas City, Missouri: Hudson-Kimberly Publishing Company, 1900. For Doniphan's legal career see Hugh P. Williamson, "Colonel Alexander W. Doniphan: Soldier, Lawyer, Statesman," *Journal of the Missouri Bar* 10 (October 1952) 180–85. For a contemporary account of Doniphan's role in the Mexican War see Frank S. Edwards, *A Campaign in New Mexico with Colonel Doniphan*. Philadelphia: Carey and Hart, 1847; reprinted 1966.

3. On July 19, 1918 the heroic statue was erected in memory of Colonel Doniphan at the courthouse square in Richmond. The statue stands ten feet tall atop a seven foot red granite pedestal. The bronzed Doniphan is gazing toward the southwest, as if looking across the western United States toward Santa Fe. An inscription on the statue reads: "On the roster of the great soldiers of the earth, must always stand in a halo of glory the name of Colonel Alexander W. Doniphan of Missouri. The county seat of Ripley County, Missouri, was named for him in 1847. Roads and schools in western Missouri are also named in his honor.

4. Given in 1884 to John Morgan, President of the Latter-day Saints Southern States Mission, Church History Library, as cited in Gregory Maynard, "Alexander William Doniphan: Man of Justice," *BYU Studies* 13.4 (Summer 1973): 472.

5. William E. Parrish, *David Rice Atchison of Missouri--Border Politician*. Columbia, Missouri: University of Missouri Press, 1961, 36–37.

6. The spelling of Doniphan has root in Donovan and may be of Irish origin even though family tradition places forebears in Spain and Scotland. Montgomery Smith Price, *The Sydney-Smith and Clagett-Price Genealogy*. Strasburg: Shenandoah Publishing House, 1927, pp. 47–100, as cited in Gregory P. Maynard, "Alexander William Doniphan, The Forgotten Man from Missouri." M.A. Thesis, Brigham Young University, August 1973, p. 1.

7. Joseph Doniphan was the son of Alexander Doniphan, who was the son of Mott Doniphan of Prince George County, Virginia. FamilySearch™.

8. He was named for his grandfathers—Alexander Doniphan and William Smith. Doniphan to Cousin Emma, Richmond, 1875, State Historical Society of Missouri, Columbia, as cited in Maynard, "Alexander William Doniphan," 2.

9. Joseph Doniphan died 12 March 12, 1813 in Mason County, Kentucky. His will dated March 2, 1813 was recorded on April 12, 1813. Named in the will were his wife, Ann F. Doniphan and seven children: Thomas Smith Doniphan, George Doniphan, Margaret Hockaday, Susanna Doniphan, Lucy Doniphan, Matilda Doniphan, and Alexander William Doniphan.

10. George Doniphan was born on July 4, 1790 and died on February 22, 1864. His wife Mary Marshall was the daughter of Chief Justice John Marshall of the Supreme Court.

11. Dewitt Clinton Allen, *Col. Alexander W. Doniphan—His Life and Character, Doniphan's Expedition*. ed. William E. Connelly. Topeka, Kansas: William E. Connelly, 1907, 21, as cited in Maynard, "Alexander William Doniphan," 4.

12. *Ibid.*, as cited in Maynard, "Alexander William Doniphan," 9.

13. *Ibid.*, 114.

14. Floyd Calvin Shoemaker, *Missouri and Missourians, Land of Contrasts and People of Achievements*. Chicago: The Lewis Publishing Co., 1943, p. 703; Dewitt Clinton Allen, *A Sketch of the Life and Character of Col. Alexander W. Doniphan*. Liberty, Missouri: Printed at the Advance Office, 1897, as cited in Joseph G. Dawson III, *Doniphan's Epic March, The 1st Missouri Volunteers in the Mexican War*, Lawrence, Kansas: University Press of Kansas, 1999, 8.

15. Inscription on Tombstone, Fairview Cemetery, Liberty, Missouri.

16. Raymond W. Settle, "Colonel Doniphan—Symbol of Pioneer Americanism." William Jewel College Bulletin, 20.7 (1947) 1–20, as cited in Maynard, "Alexander William Doniphan," 77.

17. All charges against Rigdon were dropped and he was freed from imprisonment. He left Liberty bound for Illinois on February 5, 1839. Joseph Smith, *The History of The Church of Jesus Christ of Latter-day Saints*. B. H. Roberts, ed. Salt Lake City: The Deseret Book Company, 1976, 3:69.

18. "Gen. Doniphan's Recollections of the Troubles of that Early Time," Saints' Herald 28 (August 2, 1884): 230; Kansas City Journal, June 12, 1881.

19. Smith, History of the Church, 1: 425.

20. *Times and Seasons* 6 (January 15, 1846): 1090. See Roger D. Launius, *Zion's Camp: Expedition to Missouri*, 1834. Independence, Missouri: Herald Publishing House, 1984, 144–65.

21. Smith, *History of the Church*, 2: 450.

22. The vote was 51 in favor to 11 against. Journal of the House of Representatives... First Session of the Ninth General Assembly, 373; as cited in Roger D. Launius, *Alexander William Doniphan: Portrait of a Missouri Moderate*, Columbia, Missouri: University of Missouri Press, 1997, 41. He strongly supported the Platte Purchase. He also endorsed a bill to establish the University of Missouri in December 1836 and voted in January 1837 to prohibit anti-slavery literature from entering Missouri.

23. The counties were named for Captain Matthew Caldwell, an Indian fighter from Kentucky and Colonel Joseph H. Daviess, killed in 1811 at the Battle of Tippecanoe.

24. The term "Native Americans" replaced the original text of "Indians."

25. B.H. Roberts, *Comprehensive History of The Church of Jesus Christ of Latter-day Saints*. 6 vols. Provo, Utah: BYU Press, 1965, 1: 418.

26. Journal History of the Church, January 8, 1837. Church History Library.

27. Colonel Thornton, a native of Kentucky, had been politically active in Missouri before its admission to the Union. He had been a judge in Ray County, a longtime member of the state General Assembly, and a colonel in the 28th Regiment of the Missouri Militia. Besides Jane, John Thornton and his wife Elizabeth Trigg Thornton had six daughters and a son. Conard, *Encyclopedia of the History of Missouri*, 2: 194.

28. Elizabeth Jane Thornton, eldest daughter of John and Elizabeth Thornton, was born on December 21, 1822 in Clay County, Missouri. At the double wedding held at the Baptist Church in Liberty, Jane's sister Caroline and one of Alexander's close friends, Oliver Perry Moss, from Maysville, Kentucky, were married.

29. Doniphan to Cousin Emma, Richmond, Missouri, 1875. Letters from the Joint Collection, Western Historical Manuscript Collection and State Historical Society Manuscripts. University of Missouri Library, Columbia, Missouri, as cited in "William H. Richardson's Journal of Doniphan's Expedition," *Missouri Historical Review* 22 (January 1928), 193–236; (April 1928), 331–360; (July 1928), 511–41, as cited in Maynard, "Alexander William Doniphan, A Man of Justice," 465.

30. Inscription on Tombstone, Fairview Cemetery, Liberty, Missouri.

31. Peter H. Burnett, first governor of California also lived in the house. Because the W.D. Hubbell family owned the home for many years, it was referred to as the Hubbell House. Their home was demolished in 1925. A plaque marks the site of the residence. "Missouri Mormon Frontier Foundation Newsletter," 24 (January–July 2000), 22.

32. Although a number of reasons are given for the order, many Missourians believed that Mormons moving into Daviess County was like Indians leaving the reservation. "Such a number [of Mormons] had settled in Daviess [County] that the old inhabitants were apprehensive that they would be governed soon by the revelations of the great Prophet, Joe Smith." *Western Star*, September 14, 1838, cited in Missouri Argus, September 27, 1838, as cited in Stephen C. LeSueur, *The 1838 Mormon War in Missouri*, Columbia: University of Missouri Press, 1987, 48.

33. Fourteen officers, the circuit judge Austin A. King, District Attorney Thomas C. Birch, and twenty sectarian preachers were present at the court martial. See Smith, *History of the Church*, 3: 460.

34. Sidney Rigdon affidavit, July 1, 1843, Smith, *History of the Church*, 3: 460. See Launius, *Alexander William Doniphan*, 63.

35. Smith, *History of the Church*, 3: 190.

36. *Ibid.*, 3: 191.

37. J. Wickliffe Rigdon, "I Never Knew a Time When I Did Not Know Joseph Smith," 36, as cited in Launius, *Alexander William Doniphan*, 64.

38. Lyman Wight affidavit, July 1, 1843, Smith, *History of the Church*, 3: 446. Hyrum Smith reports the same interview slightly different: "Doniphan came to us where we were under guard to shake hands and bid us farewell. 'By God, you have been sentenced by the court-martial to be shot this morning; but I will be damned if I will have any of the honor of it or any of the disgrace of it; therefore, I have ordered by brigade to take up the line of march and to leave the camp, for I consider it to be cold-blooded murder and I bid you farewell.'" "Missouri v Joseph Smith," *Times and Seasons* 3 (July 15, 1843): 251.

39. As insubordinate as his conduct was, Doniphan was never called to account for it. When the Mormon war ended, Samuel Lucas tried to induce the Governor to remove Doniphan's military commission on the grounds that he had disobeyed a superior officer. The governor refused the request.

40. "Mormon War Militia Pay Voucher," June 3, 1841, Collection #2154, folder 34, Adjutant General, Mormon War: Pay Accounts, 3d Division, Missouri Militia, 2d Addition, Nos.1–7, Officers, as cited in Launius, *Alexander William Doniphan*, 66.

41. Letter to Emma, dated Richmond 1838, as cited in Dean C. Jessee, *The Personal Writings of Joseph Smith*. Salt Lake City: Deseret Book, 1984, 368.

42. Austin A. King was born in Tennessee. He came to Richmond in 1837 from Columbia, Missouri, where he had previously practiced law. Between 1837–1848 King served as judge of Missouri's Fifth Judicial Circuit. He served as governor of Missouri from 1848–1852. In 1862 he was elected to the U.S. Congress. See *History of Ray County, Missouri*. St. Louis: Missouri Historical Co., 1881, 259-61. Conard, *Encyclopedia of the History of Missouri*, 3: 537.

43. Amos Rees was the Clay County prosecuting attorney from 1831–1834. From 1835–1837 Rees was the attorney for Missouri's Fifth Judicial Circuit. He later moved to Platte City, Missouri, and then to Fort Leavenworth, Kansas, where he continued to practice law.

44. List of the prisoners: Joseph Smith, Jun., Hyrum Smith, Sidney Rigdon, Parley P. Pratt, Lyman Wight, Amasa Lyman, George W. Robinson, Caleb Baldwin, Alanson Ripley, Washington Voorhees, Sidney Turner, John Buchanan, Jacob Gates, Chandler Holbrook, George W. Harris, Jesse D. Hunter, Andrew Whitlock, Martin C. Allred, William Allred, George D. Grant, Darwin Chase, Elijah Newman, Alvin G. Tippets, Zedekiah Owens, Isaac Morley, Thomas Beck, Moses Clawson, John J. Tanner, Daniel Shearer, Daniel S. Thomas, Alexander McRae, Elisha Edwards, John S. Higbee, Ebenezer Page, Benjamin Covey, Ebenezer Robinson, Luman Gibbs, James M. Henderson, David Pettegrew, Edward Partridge, Francis Higbee, David Frampton, George Kimball, Joseph W. Younger, Henry Zobriske, Allen J. Stout, Sheffield Daniels, Silas Maynard, Anthony Head, Benjamin Jones, Daniel Garn, John T. Earl, and Norman Shearer, as cited in Smith, *History of the Church* 3: 209.

45. E. Robinson, "Items of Person History," *The Return*, 2 (March 1890): 69. Church History Library.

46. Correspondence from John B. Clark to Lilburn W. Boggs, as cited in Leland H. Gentry, "A History of the Latter-day Saints in Northern Missouri from 1836-1839." Dissertation. Brigham Young University, 1965, 544.

47. Joseph Smith letter to Emma Smith, 12 November 1838, as cited in Jessee, *Personal Writings of Joseph Smith*, 367–68.

48. Parley P. Pratt, *Autobiography of Parley Parker Pratt*. ed. Parley P. Pratt, Jr. Salt Lake City: Deseret Book, 1968, 212.

49. Parley P. Pratt affidavit, July 1, 1843, in Smith, *History of the Church*, 3: 430.

50. Hyrum Smith affidavit, July 2, 1843, in Smith, *History of the Church*, 3: 419.

51. Joseph Smith accused Doniphan of cowardice in defending the Saints. "They have done us much harm from the beginning, they are co-workers with the mob." Joseph Smith Jr., "The Prophet's Epistle to the Church," March 25, 1839, in Smith, *History of the Church*, 3:213, 292; see Dean Jessee, *Personal Writings of Joseph Smith*, 388–407.

52. The land was located in the center of Kansas City today. Edward Partridge and Lydia Partridge, to Alexander W. Doniphan and Amos Rees, November 28, 1838 [filed 20 February 1839], Book F, 202. Church History Library; Junius F. Wells, "A Prophecy and Its Fulfillment," *Improvement Era* 6 (November 1902), 8.

53. The land was devastated during the Civil War.

54. The 1838 tax rolls of Clay County show that he owned 160 acres. The tax rolls of 1839 show an additional 320 acres.

55. Alexis de Tocqueville, Democracy in America. 2 vols. New York: 1898, 2: 342, as cited in Dawson, *Doniphan's Epic March*, 5.

56. While commander of the 1st Missouri Mounted Volunteers, he was commissioned to be a colonel in the volunteers of the U.S. Army. The army commission took precedence over the state rank.

57. The term "Native Americans" replaced the original text of "Indians."

58. Daniel Tyler, *A Concise History of the Mormon Battalion in the Mexican War*. Waynesboro, Virginia: M&R Books, 1881, 165.

59. See Dawson, *Doniphan's Epic March*, 184–202.

60. Alexander Doniphan, lawyer, Kentucky, with wife E.J. age 31 of Missouri; John age 3 years of Missouri, and James 6 months. Census Record for the Missouri, Clay County, Liberty in 1850. M432 Roll 396, 1850 Missouri, Clay County, Liberty, 301.

61. John Thornton Doniphan was born on 18 September 1838 and died on May 9, 1853 at his uncle James H. Baldwin's home in Liberty. He was looking for epsom salts for relief from a toothache and mistakenly reached for a bottle of mercury chloride, which he took to relieve his pain.

62. William Alexander Doniphan, Jr., was born on September 10, 1840 and died May 11, 1858 at age 19. He drowned in a flooded stream while a student at Bethany College in West Virginia.

63. They were educated in classical and scientific training, and were fluent in French, Spanish, German, and Italian. Doniphan to Cousin Emma, Richmond, 1875, Maynard, "Alexander William Doniphan," 23.

64. Although Doniphan and his wife were married in the Baptist Church, there is no record that he affiliated with any church until the Liberty Christian Church.

65. He was also a delegate to a secession convention called by the Missouri legislature on January 21, 1861. At that convention he presented his anti-secession views. Perhaps his efforts served a useful purpose as Missouri did not secede from the Union.

66. Only seven delegates were under age forty. Dawson, *Doniphan's Epic March*, 214.

67. The compromise did not received the support of Congress. F. Mark McKiernan and Roger D. Launius, *Missouri Folk Heroes of the 19th Century*. Independence, Missouri: Herald Publishing House, 79.

68. Allen, *A Sketch of the Life and Character of Col. Alexander W. Doniphan*, 27-8.

69. Doniphan to John Doniphan, February 22, 1861, State Historical Society of Missouri, Columbia, as cited in Maynard, "Alexander William Doniphan," 95.

70. See Dawson, *Doniphan's Epic March*, 203-24.

71. See Webb, *Battles and Biographies of Missourians*, 280.

72. Doniphan to Cousin, Richmond, May 6, 1878, in *Richardson's Journal of Doniphan's Expedition*, as cited in Maynard, "Alexander William Doniphan," 109.

73. Letter to cousin Emma, 1875 in *Richardson's Journal of Doniphan's Expedition*, as cited in Maynard, "Alexander William Doniphan," 110.

74. *Kansas City Journal* Reporter Interview, June 1, 1881, Richmond Missouri; *Kansas City Journal*, June 5, 1881, as cited in Cook, *David Whitmer Interviews*, 64.

75. Ibid., Cook, *David Whitmer Interviews*, 70.

76. John Morgan Diary, Church History Library; see Arthur M. Richardson and Nicholas G. Morgan, Sr., *The Life and Ministry of John Morgan*. Salt Lake City: Nicholas G. Morgan, Sr., 1965, 323, as cited in Cook, *David Whitmer Interview*, 90.

77. Interview of Heman C. Smith and William H. Kelley, June 19, 1884, *Saints' Herald*, 31 (July 12, 1884), as cited in Cook, *David Whitmer Interview*, 133.

CHAPTER 5

Alexander W. Doniphan, Fort Leavenworth and Mexican American War

Kelvin Crow

From the Center for Military History, an outline of the key activities of Alexander W. Doniphan's activities at Fort Leavenworth leading up to his campaign in the Mexican War.

Chapter Page Image: Missouri's Mounted Volunteers lead by Doniphan in a highly stylized lithograph depicting the Battle of Sacramento. -- *Currier, N. (1847). The Battle of Sacramento: Fought February 28th 1847 [New York: N. Currier] Photograph found in Popular Graphic Arts, Library of Congress, Washington. Retrieved July, 2020, from https://www.loc.gov/item/90709394/ (Originally photographed 1847)*

Information Paper

ATZL-CMH
5 Mar 2020

1. Purpose. To provide background on the subject.

2. Facts.

    a. The Mexican American War of 1846–47 was caused by the admission of Texas into the Union and disagreement over the southern border of that state. American strategy was initially to seize the disputed territory and compel Mexico to negotiate by taking California and New Mexico. After this failed, the strategy evolved to attacking the northern provinces and eventually capturing the capital.

    b. On May 13, 1846 Congress voted to raise 50,000 twelve-month volunteers for service in the conflict. Missouri Governor John Edwards asked Doniphan, a brigadier general in the militia and a state representative, to raise 2 companies (120 men) of mounted volunteers in the western counties. This he did, departing for Fort Leavenworth on June 4, 1846 and arriving on the June 6. Doniphan enlisted as a private. The soldiers provided their own weapons, equipment, and horses. They were sworn in on June 7 as Company C, First Missouri Mounted Volunteer Regiment. Many more soldiers arrived eventually raising the regiment to 856 men in 8 companies.

    c. The regulars at Fort Leavenworth set up school to teach both warfare and camp survival. The school was not popular with the volunteers but brigadier generals Kearney and Doniphan both did their best to accommodate and educate the rough frontiersmen. School was held in morning and afternoon sessions. Assuming they trained every day, it was just over two weeks of instruction.

d. Elections for officers was held on June 18, and Doniphan was selected as regimental commander by a majority of 500 votes over his opponent. While he did not overtly campaign, his backers provided liquor to the troops. His principle subordinates were West Pointers. Kearney briefed Doniphan on his mission and gave him military textbooks that he studied, "at every leisure moment."

e. Kearny gave a great deal of thought to logistics, but his preparations were insufficient. He amassed 1,556 wagons, almost 15,000 cattle, and 459 Army horses; he sent wagons and hunters ahead to preposition supplies, and staged his forces along the route to allow forage, water, and game to restock between elements. He planned to sustain 1,300 men for three months, but conditions along the 500-mile march to the border were scant and at times desperate. Inexperience, heat, and rough conditions killed animals and broke equipment.

f. The second half of the march was harder. After a week's rest at Bent's Fort, the troops crossed a desert then climbed the Rocky Mountains to a 7,754-foot pass. By the time Doniphan's men reached that point, half their horses had died. Kearney asked Doniphan's advice as a lawyer on how to naturalize the new citizens they were to encounter on August 15, and Doniphan composed the oath. The unit arrived in Santa Fe, at the end of a 1,000-mile march, on August 18.

g. In Santa Fe, Doniphan oversaw the construction of a fort and a committee drafting a legal code for the new territory. Blending Spanish and American traditions, it was officially adopted September 22, 1846. When Kearney left for California, Doniphan attempted to negotiate peace treaties with the Navajo and Zuni tribes.

h. On December 14, 1846 Doniphan dispatched his first elements into Chihuahua province. After crossing the desert Jornada del Muerto (Journey of the Dead), they encountered a superior force at El Brazito. Doniphan had his soldiers squat or lie down and hold their fire until the Mexicans were at close range, then deliver 2 volleys and charge. The Mexicans fled with 43 killed and 150 wounded to Doniphan's 7 wounded. The battle was over in about 30 minutes.

i. The First Missouri prepared defensive positions on February 28, 1847 before Chihuahua City. Although reinforced with light artillery, Doniphan was still outnumbered. But through good reconnaissance he identified the weakness of the positions and maneuvered to flank them. The Mexican forces lost about 700 killed in the Battle of Sacramento to one officer killed in Doniphan's unit.

j. Doniphan occupied the capital from March 1 to April 28, 59 days of garrison duty that nearly ruined the force, then marched to join General Taylor at Saltillo.

k. Doniphan rendezvoused with the main body on May 22, 1847 to an incredulous reception. The rest of the Army had almost forgotten they existed. The Missourians were unkempt and ill-uniformed but clearly maintained a fighting spirit. 10 June 10, the unit departed for New Orleans where they were celebrated and accepted discharge. Return thence to home was at their own expense.

l. Doniphan's March of almost 4,000 miles across mountains, deserts, and rivers is rightly compared to Xenophon's Anabasis. Whatever his luck in having unskilled opponents, his slashing one-sided victories in Chihuahua still almost defy imagination. His conquest of northwestern Mexico led to the territories' inclusions into the U.S. and his occupation of Chihuahua gave an important bargaining chip to the victor in the eventual peace negotiations.

CHAPTER 6

Alexander W. Doniphan "American Xenophon"

Allen Jones

A brief recount of Alexander W. Doniphan's expedition during the Mexican War, from enlistment through his triumphant return to Liberty.

Chapter Page Image: Portraits taken in 1888 of the surviving members of Captain A.P. Moss' (2) Company serving under Doniphan (1) in the Mexican War. -- *1st Regiment Missouri Volunteers Veterans [Photograph found in Photograph Collection, State Historical Society of Missouri, Columbia]. (1888). Retrieved July, 2020, from https://digital.shsmo.org/digital/collection/imc/id/20296/rec/3 (Doniphan, Alexander W. (Col.). Moss, O.P. (Capt.). Sublett, L.B. (1st Lieut.). Moss, Jas. H.(2nd Lieut.). McCarty, Thos. (1st Sarg.). McClintock, A.K. (2nd Sarg.). Wallis, George H. (Corporal). Groom, Jno. S. Warren, John. Pence, W.H. Campbell)*

Nicknamed the "American Xenophon" after the ancient Greek military commander who led Grecian soldiers on a long and arduous march against Persia, Colonel Alexander W. Doniphan commanded troops in one of the longest military marches in history and fought in several successful battles during the Mexican-American War (1846–1848), proving himself to be an inspiring leader and adept military commander.

On April 25, 1846, Mexican cavalry attacked U.S. Soldiers during a border skirmish near the Rio Grande. Newly elected President James K. Polk had sent the soldiers to the disputed region to pressure Mexico after it refused to sell California and New Mexico. Tensions between the two countries were already strained after the U.S. admitted Texas, which had declared its independence from Mexico just a few years earlier, into the Union in 1845. The presence of U.S. troops in Mexico's territory was a tipping point. Polk used the attack near the Rio Grande to his advantage, and on May 13, 1846, the U.S. declared war on Mexico and authorized the recruitment of 50,000 volunteer soldiers.

During this same time, in western Missouri, Doniphan's law practice was flourishing, and he had just finished serving two terms in the state legislature. While attending the Ray County Circuit Court in May 1846, Doniphan received a letter from Governor John C. Edwards requesting Doniphan to help raise companies of volunteers to fight in the war. Doniphan went to work immediately and began delivering rousing speeches around Missouri, calling for volunteers. Many heeded his persuasive call to arms.

The volunteer recruits assembled at Fort Leavenworth and were organized into eight companies of the First Missouri Mounted

Volunteer Regiment. Although Doniphan had served as the brigadier general of the Western division of the Missouri Militia in the late 1830s, he volunteered to serve as a private in the regular army to fight shoulder to shoulder with his fellow volunteers. Doniphan was in company C from Liberty.

On June 18, 1846, the Missouri Mounted Volunteers held elections to determine their officers—the men who would lead them in war. Despite never having led troops into battle, Doniphan was elected colonel with a near unanimous vote and reported directly to colonel, and soon to be Brigadier General Stephen W. Kearny of the regular U.S. Army.

Colonel Kearny was leading the Army of the West, which in addition to the Missouri Volunteers included two regular army regiments from Fort Leavenworth, the 1st Calvary Regiment, an artillery and infantry battalion, and later the Mormon Battalion, the only religious unit in American military history. Kearny's Army of the West totaled about 1,700 men, and the Missouri Volunteers made up about half of that force with over 850 men.

The Missouri Volunteers were a rowdy and spirited group of mostly farm boys that could be difficult to control. Although ordered to wear specific clothing as uniforms, the volunteers rarely complied stating that they joined to fight, not dress pretty. Even Doniphan preferred to wear plain clothing rather than a military uniform. Doniphan did, however, wear a distinctive broad-rimmed white hat.

After a few weeks of training at Fort Leavenworth, the Army of the West began their long march through disputed Indian territory to seize Santa Fe. Two advance companies departed on June 22, 1846. The first group of Missouri Mounted Volunteers left four days later, and Colonel Doniphan and his remaining volunteers departed on June 29. The following day, Kearny was promoted to brigadier general, and he and his remaining army commenced their march toward Mexico. The departures were staggered to not overtax waters sources and grass for the livestock.

The march to Santa Fe was grueling. Kearny pushed the men to average about 20 miles a day to move as rapidly as possible. Natural obstacles were a constant challenge with deep ravines, creeks with high and rugged banks, rivers too deep to cross, uneven terrain that broke axles, and soft prairie ground that became quicksand for heavy wagons. All of this took an exhausting toll on the men and draft animals and slowed their advance.

Additionally, as recorded by Private Jacob S. Robinson, a recruit in the Missouri Volunteers, "Thirst was a constant companion on the sun-drenched prairies, while the men often went hungry whenever their commissary wagons fell far behind." The men endured torrential rains, withering heat, low rations, and sickness. Even Kearny became ill and had to ride in a wagon for a time. Many of the horses died, forcing the men to walk, and the trail was often marked with the blood of their feet. Doniphan's horse, Bucephalus, died about a week after leaving Fort Leavenworth, but luckily, Doniphan brought a second horse allowing him to remain astride inspiring the volunteers to continue.

Six hundred miles from Fort Leavenworth, the Army of the West united at Bent's Fort in southeastern Colorado in late July. Bent's Fort was a large self-contained community established as a trading post. Approaching the fort, the volunteers could see a large

U.S. flag waiving in the wind, which raised the morale of the men. While waiting for each of Kearny's units to arrive, the volunteers rested and participated in drills, and the officers devised strategies for taking Santa Fe. They would soon cross into foreign territory ready for war.

The governor of Santa Fe, Manuel Armijo, learned of the advancing U.S. Army in late June and sent a request to Mexico asking for regular troops to help defend Santa Fe. Although Mexican officials promised to send troops, none arrived. On August 8, Governor Armijo issued a proclamation to the people of New Mexico, ordering them to prepare to defend their country. On August 15, Armijo assembled an army of about 3,000 men and marched to Apache Canyon, about 15 miles from Santa Fe. There they built a strong position with fortifications and six cannons. Nevertheless, many of Armijo's men did not want to fight. There was confusion, fear, and in-fighting causing numbers of militiamen to desert. As a result, Armijo disbanded his large army and fled before he ever saw the Army of the West.

As the volunteers marched through Apache Canyon, prepared to fight, they were no doubt grateful to find the fortifications abandoned. Doniphan remarked, "Five hundred good men could have kept us there until Christmas."

Without a single shot fired, the Army of the West took Santa Fe on August 18, 1846. Kearny immediately ordered the raising of the U.S. flag. Bugles sounded and cannons fired signifying the first U.S. conquest of foreign lands by military force. Kearny then took a large part of the army and marched to outlying towns to inform them of the U.S. occupation.

Doniphan was left in charge as acting governor of Santa Fe, and using his skills as a lawyer, he began drafting a code of laws for the new U.S. territory. The code was finished in about a month and comprised 115 double-columned pages written in English and Spanish. Many years later, Doniphan remarked:

> It is astonishing, considering the short time we had been there and our limited means of information, that we should have written a code that Congress after the annexation of the territory, re-enacted and which, after thirty-five years I found still in vogue in 1881.

Soon thereafter, Kearny departed for California leaving Doniphan with his Missouri Volunteers. Doniphan would continue to act as governor until Colonel Sterling W. Price arrived in Santa Fe, at which time Doniphan was to take his volunteers north into Navajo country to enter into a peace treaty with the Native Americans and then south to help with the capture of Chihuahua.

Shortly after Kearny's departure, the Mormon Battalion entered Santa Fe. Doniphan ordered a 100-gun salute to welcome the beleaguered battalion and likely to thank them for their loyalty and dedication to the U.S. despite the wrongs they had suffered. To support the U.S., these men had left their families who were struggling to travel west because of persecution. Despite the unpopularity of the members of The Church of Jesus Christ of Latter-day Saints in Missouri, Doniphan had always shown them respect and support. Doniphan was happy to see old friends and acquaintances among the tired and sick soldiers. The Mormon Battalion was to rest and then continue to California to meet up with Kearny, building a wagon road along the way. They would march nearly 2,000 miles before heading back to be with their families.

On October 29, 1846, Colonel Price arrived in Santa Fe, allowing Doniphan to prepare to go north. He was to enter into a peace treaty and convince the Native Americans to stop raiding nearby settlements, now under U.S. control. The plan was to divide Doniphan's forces into three units, search for and round up all the Navajo chiefs, and then rendezvous at Bear Springs on November 20 for treaty negotiations.

After much difficulty searching for the Native Americans, on November 21, 1846, Doniphan met with fourteen Navajo chiefs including Chief Narbona and about 500 other Navajo. Doniphan informed the Navajo that New Mexico now belonged to the U.S. and that the Navajo and the Mexicans were "children of the United States." Doniphan further declared that they would protect the Mexicans from any attack by the Navajo, but that the U.S. desired to enter into a treaty of peace and friendship with the Navajo. Doniphan's boldness impressed the Native Americans who agreed to the treaty and returned prisoners they had recently taken.

After successfully completing his mission among the Navajo, Doniphan began his march south toward El Paso and Chihuahua City. Doniphan and his volunteers had to cross the inhospitable Jornada del Muerto (Spanish for "Journey of the Dead"), a barren desert nearly 100 miles long. Crossing this dangerous terrain took five days maintaining a moderate pace for 16 hours a day. The men again suffered thirst, hunger, and fatigue and the volunteers went without hot food or fire for lack of wood.

On December 25, Doniphan and his volunteers reached a bend in the Rio Grande called El Brazito, which is about 30 miles north of El Paso. Since it was Christmas Day, Doniphan halted his men around 1 p.m. and allowed them to set up camp, rest, and wait for stragglers. Men scattered looking for wood and water. Doniphan and some officers sat down under a tree to play a card game called three-trick-loo as a fun way to help settle a dispute over a horse.

Suddenly, a large dust cloud appeared on the horizon approaching the camp. An army of about 1,000 Mexican soldiers under the command of Major Antonio Ponce de Leon were closing in on the unprepared Missouri Volunteers. Ponce's army consisted of the Chihuahua Infantry, the El Paso Militia, the Zacatecas Dragoons, and the Veracruz Lancers. The soldiers wore spectacular uniforms, which consisted of green coats trimmed in red and tall hats with horsehair plumes—quite the contrast from the non-uniformed, coarse looking Missourians. The Mexicans were also heavily armed and ready for battle.

Undaunted, Doniphan laid down his cards, ordered the bugle sounded, mounted his horse, and began organizing his men—at least those who were around. In less than five minutes, the Mexican troops were in sight. The Missouri Mounted Volunteers dropped whatever they were doing, ran back to camp, grabbed their weapons, and set up a defensive line on foot because there was no time to collect their horses.

Only about 500 volunteers were close enough to be in formation when the Mexicans sent a messenger forward carrying a black flag with a white skull and crossbones. The Mexican lieutenant demanded that Doniphan and his men surrender. When the volunteers refused, the Mexican lieutenant exclaimed, "Prepare for a charge! We neither ask nor give quarter!" Doniphan shot back "Charge and be damned!" Despite being heavily outnumbered, the lawyer from Missouri, with no military training or battle experience, was calm and sure.

When the messenger returned to his line, the entire Mexican force made a bold charge. Doniphan galloped around his men, shouting encouragement and ordered them to lay low and not return fire until the opposing force was about 60 yards away. He yelled to "Remember Okeechobee" reminding them of the disgraceful retreat of the Missouri Volunteers in the Florida Indian war nine years before. Today was the day to erase that disgrace from Missouri history.

Ponce's army fired ragged volleys, and they cheered wildly. When the Mexicans saw volunteers lying on the ground, which was entirely unconventional, they assumed they had hit their marks boosting their morale. In reality, they had missed horribly. Doniphan continued to order his men to take their fire and remain still. In his after-action report, Doniphan stated that "three rounds were fired by the whole [Mexican] line, also from a two-pound howitzer, before they had advanced within rifle shot."

When the advancing army was about 60 yards away, Doniphan gave the command to fire, which occurred with devastating accuracy. Ponce's soldiers were dismayed and confused by the "dead" Americans rising and taking shots while the Mexicans tried to reload. The deadly volleys from the volunteers broke the enemy's charge and threw them into chaos.

Most of the shots from the Mexican dragoons were wild and fell on a hill where Doniphan was directing the battle behind some of his men, and he later wrote: "Their shot was falling thick around me. I put spurs to my horse charged to the front, hollered 'Come on boys.'.…The boys thought I was brave as hell, but they did not know what drove me there."

The Mexican lancers attempted to flank the volunteers but were stopped by a volley from the teamsters on their wagons. Captain John Reid then lead eighteen horsemen into the battle with a saber charge. After another volley from Doniphan's men, the Mexican's were in a full retreat.

Although vicious, the entire battle lasted only thirty minutes. The Missourians had 8 wounded, none killed. The Mexicans had 151 wounded, including Ponce, 71 killed, and 15 taken prisoners. The volunteers captured supplies, the howitzer, and hampers of wine. Doniphan's first battle was a decisive victory, and that Christmas night, the Missourians wined and dined on their spoils of war.

After the battle, Doniphan and his officers finished their card game, but the disputed horse had escaped. Doniphan wrote in his official report of the battle: "I cannot speak too highly of the coolness and intrepid bravery of the officers and men under my command during this whole engagement," and also noted, "few of them had ever been in battle before."
Fully expecting another battle, Doniphan took El Paso without a fight and raised the U.S. flag on December 27. The following day he told the citizens that "he did not come to plunder and ravage, but to offer them liberty and protection." He also prohibited his men from stealing from the community and encouraged the locals to sell goods to his men. Doniphan understood that the business opportunity for the locals would help ease tensions.

The volunteers spent a few weeks resting while Doniphan prepared to go south to assist General John E. Wool and his men in the capture of Chihuahua. However, Doniphan learned that General Wool's plans had changed, and he was no longer marching to Chihuahua. Without new orders, Doniphan now had to decide whether to head back north or continue south with only his men, knowing he would be greatly outnumbered.

Doniphan was determined to take Chihuahua, but he understood the risks and that he was leading a group of volunteers without clear orders from Kearny. Out of great respect to his men, Doniphan explained the situation and allowed them to vote on what direction they should go. United and inspired by their commander, the volunteers voted to take Chihuahua. These men now owned the decision to fight.

Prior to leaving El Paso, Major Meriwether Lewis Clark, son of William Clark, arrived with a company of light artillery with 6 cannons on February 1, 1847. This addition increased Doniphan's force to almost 1,000 men, and on February 8, they marched south.

Having already traveled over 1,000 miles, the volunteers were once again marching through arid and inhospitable territory, facing another 300 miles of thirst and heat. Going further into enemy territory, the men were now under even greater stress as they were constantly on the lookout for an ambush. Despite knowing the march would end with a battle against a superior force, Doniphan and his men marched with haste and confidence.

On February 27, scouts reported to Doniphan that the Mexicans were entrenched about 15 miles from Chihuahua on the Sacramento River. Nearly four thousand Mexican troops under

Governor Angel Trias Alvarez and experienced officers including Generals Jose A. Heredia and Garcia Conde were ready for battle. The Mexican troops included 1,200 cavalry, 1,500 infantry, and 119 artillerymen with 10 field guns and 6 culverins, and 1,000 rancheros (Mexican volunteers). As expected, Doniphan's force was heavily outnumbered—four to one.

Despite the numbers, Doniphan and his men were just as calm and sure as they had been at El Brazito. His strategy for attack was a tactic used in Indian country. Wagons were organized into four parallel columns with his troops between the wagons. They moved slowly toward the Mexican lines. Knowing the enemy's position was too strong for a direct attack, Doniphan suddenly swung his force to the west and up a hill. A strategic move unexpected by the Mexican commanders. Nevertheless, the Mexican Calvary charged with support from infantry and artillery, but their charge was quickly halted by Major Clark's artillery.

In response, the Mexican artillery opened fire, which started a 50-minute artillery duel. While the volunteers were able to dodge the cannon balls fired from the Mexican artillery, Major Clark's artillery was far more deadly and accurate at inflicting heavy causalities. Doniphan calmly sat astride his horse and whittled throughout the duel waiting for the right time to advance.

As the Mexicans fell back to regroup, Doniphan ordered his entire force to advance yelling, "Let her rip!" The Mexican artillery attempted to stop the advance but proved ineffective. The volunteers charged forward and showed great courage in overtaking redoubts and other fortifications. The advance could not be stopped. After numerous clashes and even some hand-to-hand fighting, the Mexicans fled. Attempts to regroup were thwarted by Clark's artillery. Doniphan's charge was fast and furious and despite being incredibly outnumbered, the Mexican army of 4,000 retreated.

The Battle of Sacramento River lasted less than four hours. Doniphan and his men were victorious against a force four times their size who had the advantage of artillery, elevation, and strong fortifications. Incredibly, Doniphan reported at least 600 Mexicans killed and wounded, plus 40 prisoners. In contrast, the U.S. lost 1 man who was killed and had 11 wounded. The volunteers also captured all the artillery, equipment, weapons, ammunition, and food of the Mexicans. The victors also found the black skull and crossbones flag the Mexicans carried at the Battle of Brazito.

Doniphan paraded his volunteers through the nearly empty city of Chihuahua on March 2, 1847. Upon learning of Doniphan's success, President Polk wrote in his diary: "The Battle of Sacramento I consider to be one of the most decisive and brilliant achievements of the war."

After some much needed rest and recuperation, Doniphan and his men were to report to Saltillo and then return to the U.S. on boats through the Gulf. Their enlistments were up, and they were going home having served their country honorably. This still meant at least two more weeks of marching. The city of Chihuahua was officially returned to Mexico on May 1, 1847. Doniphan had completed every order and mission he had been tasked with.

Doniphan arrived in St. Louis, Missouri on July 2, 1847, where the citizens held a parade and reception to honor and welcome home the heroes. On July 15, Liberty held a celebration for Doniphan that attracted more than 8,000 people and lasted all day.

The American Xenophon, who left his law practice to volunteer to go to war, lead his men over 5,000 miles, through forbidding and hostile territory. He rounded up hostile Native Americans and convinced them to enter into a peace treaty, which allowed U.S. forces to concentrate on the war. He served as the acting governor of Santa Fe and wrote a code of laws for the new territory, which was utilized for over 30 years. He bravely led his men into two battles defeating superior forces—one significantly so—and he never wavered from the orders he received.

Most importantly, after all they had gone through, the Private who was voted to be the Colonel of the First Regiment of the Missouri Mounted Volunteers was loved and respected by his men. Private William H. Richardson wrote this of his beloved commander:

> The man who can familiarize himself with the poorest private, by some kind word, or ride among the troops, and make us forget that we were hungry or thirsty, by some pleasant converse, in our long and toilsome march; -- the man who can forget his own personal safety in the hour of danger, and rise superior to every embarrassment—who can be prepared for every emergency by superior skill in the tactics of war—as well as refined sense of honor, and an open suavity of manner not only leading captive the hearts of his entire command, but those of the hostile foe—such a man is a treasure to society, and how to his country—and such a man is the brave Doniphan.

Sources Consulted

Doniphan's Epic March, The 1st Missouri Volunteers in the Mexican War, by Joseph G. Dawson, III, June 28, 1999

The Encyclopedia of the Mexican-American War, A Political, Social, and Military History, by Spencer C. Tucker, 2013

Doniphan's Expedition and the Conquest of New Mexico and California, By John Taylor Hughes, William Elsey Connelley, Dewitt Clinton Allen, Charles R. Morehead, August 22, 2015

Alexander William Doniphan, The Forgotten Man From Missouri, by Gregory P. Maynard, August 1973

Alexander William Doniphan, Portrait of a Missouri Moderate, by Roger D. Launius, 1997

Trail Dust: Chronicles of Kearney's Expedition to Santa Fe, by Mare Simmons for The New Mexican, July 7, 2012

Journal of William H. Richardson, by William Richardson, 1848

CHAPTER 7

Music Perhaps Unheard in 150 Years Plays Sunday

Jack "Miles" Ventimiglia,
Editor, The Sun Newspapers May 31, 2000

Originally printed in The Sun Newspapers on May 31, 2000, this article explains the story of the Doniphan March, a musical score written to celebrate the return of the Missouri Volunteers from their campaign in Mexico, how it was lost for decades, found in an archive at Yale University, and played in Liberty, Missouri about 150 years after its composition.

Chapter Page Image: Cover for the sheet music for "Col. Doniphan's Grand March."
-- Waldauer, A., & Beinecke, F. W. (circa 1848). Col. Doniphan's Grand March [Lithograph and sheet music published in St. Louis by Buford & Co.]. Retrieved July, 2020, from Beinecke Rare Book and Manuscript Library, Yale University https://brbl-dl.library.yale.edu/vufind/Record/4087097

A lively march, perhaps not heard in public for more than 150 years, will help mark the dedication of the Alexander Doniphan house site in Liberty on June 4.

St. Louis Theater conductor A. Waldouer composed the "Col. Doniphan Grand March" to play in July 1848. He composed the march for a St. Louis celebration of Doniphan and the Missouri volunteers who had fought in Mexico.

Doniphan returned to Missouri from the Mexican War by way of the Gulf of Mexico and the Mississippi River.
During the St. Louis celebration, Doniphan spoke to a crowd that had gathered to honor him. Doniphan gave the honor to his men.

"Your noble, heroic conduct on the battlefields of Brazito and Sacramento will ever be remembered with gratitude by your countrymen. NO peculiar generalship was displayed in these battles. If ever the rank and file of the army should have the honor of a victory, such should be the case at the battle of Sacramento," Doniphan said, according to a Liberty Tribune period article. "At the battlefield, we found the enemy. You were marched until you came in view of the enemy's redoubts planted with cannon. You were told that there was the enemy. You were marched until within the proper distance when you turned loose! The enemy first recoiled, then gave, then fled. The charge was impetuous. The battle was won! It was yours."

The enthusiastic crowd cheered Doniphan, heard speeches in his honor, and listened to the march composed by Waldouer. After the music faded, someone filed away the composition—presumably it had met its purpose and that was that.

Until earlier this year when Liberty resident Chad Means discovered a footnote in a book that described the St. Louis celebration. When the idea of honoring Doniphan surfaced, Means said he began researching the Mexican War history and found a reference in a book to the music composed for Doniphan.

"I tracked it to the rare manuscript collection at Yale University Library," Means said.

Means who does not read music, said he has not heard the music and has no idea whether it has been heard by anyone since it rang in Doniphan's ears in 1848.

"I don't know whether it's fast-paced," Means said. "I have been curious since we first received it to know whether it was brass band–type music, but the indication now is it was written and intended for piano. I can't imagine what it's like, and next Sunday may be one of the first times it will have been played in over 150 years."

Calvin Permenter, a William Jewell music instructor, will play the march at the dedication. As expected in a march, there is repetition to it, but the "intermediate level" music also is creative, Permenter said.

"Col. Doniphan Grand March" is among several parts to an event being held in recognition of Doniphan starting at 3:30 p.m. Sunday, June 4, at the Presbyterian Church, Main and Mississippi Streets, Liberty.

The main event involves the dedication of a plaque marking the site of the residence, on Main Street, where Doniphan once lived.

The Doniphan Chapter of the Daughters of the American Revolution purchased the plaque with the aid of a $2,700 donation from Kansas City 150 Legacy Fund.

Liberty Mayor Steve Hawkins and the event organizer, Councilwoman Juarenne Hester, will appear, and Dr. Joseph G. Dawson III, a Texas A&M history professor and author of a book on Doniphan, will give remarks. Dawson said Doniphan is a historically important figure whose significance became overshadowed by the onset of the Civil War.

Several descendants of the Doniphan marchers, including the one-hundred-year-old Florence Merchant, said they plan to attend the event. Merchant is the granddaughter of march member Joseph Addison Smith, whom she called "a nice man" that she got to know during her school-age years.
Following the plaque dedication, an outdoor reception will be held at the Presbyterian Church courtyard.

After the reception, a dinner will be held at Yates College Union. Dawson will provide a talk about Doniphan. Reservations cost $15 and may be made by calling 781-7700, Ext. 5376.

"(Dawson) has done research into and written about specific aspects of Doniphan's march," Hester said. "We did not know we would be able to get someone so well qualified to speak on this subject."

The Times of Alexander William Doniphan

CHAPTER 8

Pick a Side: Doniphan's Role in Missouri's Loyalty to the Union

Kathleen Bird, JD

A history of the life of Alexander Doniphan taking time to compare his life with that of his law partner and contemporary, David Rice Atchison. Doniphan and Atchison were sometimes of like mind but more often were not.

Chapter Page Image: Bust of Alexander Doniphan amongst other famous and noteworthy Missourians in the State Capitol. -- *Morgan, J. (2020, April 20). Bust of Alexander Doniphan [Photograph]. Capitol of the State of Missouri, Jefferson City, MO.*

The election of Abraham Lincoln as president of the U.S. instigated events that forced residents of Missouri to carefully choose allegiances that would impact their physical and financial well-being for a decade or more. Friends and neighbors who had co-existed peacefully over previous decades, embracing common hopes for Missouri's future prosperity, found their relationships profoundly tested as opposing factions demanded loyalty to their point of view.

People looked to community leaders for knowledgeable advice. In western Missouri, Alexander William Doniphan and David Rice Atchison were among those who were vocal in shaping public opinion. They shared a common heritage and cultural values and had been friends and colleagues prior to these events. Their projections of the future consequences of their choices, however, led to diverging viewpoints on the appropriate course of action, moving them into opposing camps. Alexander Doniphan held out hope that a united nation could survive the polarizing issues of the day. David Rice Atchison became an activist for one side, using his influence in ways that disrupted the western side of the state, leading to death, destruction, and mayhem. It is striking how themes of patriotism, commonality, and the rule of law, debated in their day, are again a focus of public discourse.

Alexander Doniphan was the youngest of ten children, born on July 9, 1808 in Kentucky. His parents were from Virginia and migrated to Kentucky with Daniel Boone, eventually settling in Mason County, where his father became Sheriff. Doniphan lost his father when he was five and was taken under the wing of an older brother to receive his education. Doniphan's tutor, Richard Keene, exposed Doniphan to the ideas of the Enlightenment and principles of moderation and devotion to rational thinking, which he embraced throughout his life. After college, Doniphan read the law for two years in the office of Martin P. Marshall, brother of Chief Justice John Marshall of the U.S. Supreme Court, who encouraged him to appreciate the evolution of our legal system and the law of law over the will of autocrats. Doniphan was admitted to the bar in Kentucky and Ohio, then decided to link his fortunes to growth on the frontier. At six-foot-four-inches, with thick auburn hair, he was a striking figure.[1]

David Rice Atchison has also been born in Kentucky on August 11, 1807. His grandfather was an immigrant from Ireland. David stood over six feet tall at maturity and was reportedly a jovial man with simple tastes who was sympathetic to the interests of the common man. In school he acquired a taste of theatrics and often entertained his friends with his acting. Jefferson Davis, a classmate at Transylvania University, remembered Atchison as a man of unswerving courage and stainless honor. He studied law for several years in Kentucky, then set out for Missouri in 1830. A flamboyant personality and energetic orator, his reputation as a lawyer grew quickly. Atchison had an established law practice in Liberty by the time Doniphan arrived in Missouri.[2]

The future of the two men overlapped for a while. Doniphan rode the Fifth Judicial Circuit from county to county with other lawyers, seeking clients and developing his reputation. He became acquainted with Atchison, who he admired as a more accomplished practitioner. By 1833, they were sharing office space in Liberty. The two hunted, played cards, and served in the local militia together. Doniphan thought Atchison was "a very ripe scholar … [with a] clear, bright, logical mind … at trial the position he took in any case he sustained with ability, and when he was on the right side, he rarely failed of success."[3] Doniphan also established a fine reputation as an orator. His eloquence was "beyond description," in the opinion of a local businessman, who suggested Doniphan would be counted among the greatest orators that ever lived.[4]

Doniphan and Atchison's relationship in the 1830s was amicable and their goals mutual. They jointly represented the legal interests of the Mormon residents of Jackson County who were being expelled from Independence, and they were involved in many negotiations to quell disturbances between their clients and other residents. They were successful in securing a new settlement for their clients northern Missouri. As commander of a Division of the State Militia, Atchison did his best to quell clashes between Mormons and other settlers after the resettlement in Daviess County. Governor Boggs received numerous complaints that Atchison was too conciliatory toward the Mormons. Boggs ordered General Clark to lead troops to drive these "enemies" from the state, and to "exterminate" them if necessary. Doniphan, who was present when Joseph Smith was captured, intervened in Clark's plan for summary execution of the Mormon leader and escorted Smith to the Liberty Jail to insure he received due process.[5]

By the mid-1830s, the political viewpoints of Doniphan and Atchison began to diverge. In 1834, Atchison was elected to the Missouri House of Representatives with the support of his Mormon clients and friends. During that session he was instrumental in pushing for the annexation of the Platte Purchase to extend the western boundary of the state. The area of the proposed Platte Purchase on the western side of the border of the U.S. and in Native American Territory. The proposal caused a legal problem as the Missouri Compromise of 1820 prohibited the expansion of slavery into new territory. It also violated the Indian

Removal Act of 1830 that committed the U.S. to respect tribal lands west of Missouri in perpetuity. Atchison saw these laws as impediments to westward expansion by slaveholders. Farmers in western Missouri relied on hemp as their cash crop, which required labor provided by their slaves. Expansion west would best suit them if slavery was expanded too. Atchison actively pushed for revocation of the Missouri Compromise, a move that would destabilize the border and ignite violent unrest among residents of Missouri and Kansas.

Atchison aligned himself with the Democratic Party, while Doniphan became more active in the Whig Party. When Atchison decided not to run for re-election to the state legislature in 1836, Doniphan ran and was elected as a Whig to replace him. Atchison was subsequently appointed as the first circuit judge for the new Twelfth Circuit, made up of Platte and Clinton counties. Doniphan practiced before Judge Atchison, rode the circuit with him, and continued to socialize with him. In 1843, the Democrats wanted Atchison to run for governor, but he refused. Later he was appointed to replace one of Missouri's U.S. Senators who died.[6]

Atchison used his time in Congress to campaign for popular sovereignty.[7] Proponents argued that the residents of new territories to be annexed to the U.S. should decide for themselves whether the territory should permit slavery or enter the Union as a free state. Atchison encouraged Senator Stephen A. Douglas of Illinois to sponsor the Kansas-Nebraska Act, which would undo the Missouri Compromise. Atchison's increasing influence in the Democratic party led to his election as Senate President Pro Tempore in 1845. He was then only thirty-eight years old.

In the meantime, Doniphan grew in personal wealth and stature. He did not actively participate in the push for popular sovereignty. He married well, cementing his connection to John Thornton, a fellow legislator and successful businessman in Clay County. The wedding was a double ceremony for his bride and her sister, who married Oliver P. Moss. Moss would later become one of Doniphan's political allies. Doniphan's law practice flourished. He engaged in land speculation, banking, and railroad development.

Upon the outbreak of the Mexican War in 1846, Doniphan was commissioned as a Colonel of the First Missouri Mounted Volunteer Regiment. During the war, his efforts were sometimes coordinated with Colonel Sterling Price, who would later serve as Governor of Missouri from 1853 to 1857 and become an advocate of secession. Doniphan's military accomplishments, including the capture of Santa Fe and the invasion of New Mexico, resulted in Doniphan and his troops returning home to a hero's welcome. When Abraham Lincoln later met Doniphan, he was eager to shake Doniphan's, exclaiming that Doniphan certainly met his expectations of a war hero.[8]

Doniphan's health suffered as a result of his service in the Mexican War, but he continued engaging in civic activities, such as drafting a civil code for New Mexico that served as the basis for the state's Bill of Rights, working for the establishment of William Jewell College, and serving as the first superintendent of Clay County schools. Unfortunately, this period ended with several personal tragedies. His eldest son died of accidental poisoning and his remaining son drown in a flood. His wife suffered a stroke that left her semi-invalid for the rest of her life.

Atchison continued to push the cause of popular sovereignty wholeheartedly. Passage of the Kansas-Nebraska Act in 1854 emboldened him to act. Atchison believed that the prosperity or the ruin of the whole South depended on the Kansas question, where abolitionists from the north were packing the state to vote as Free Soilers. In 1855, he decided not to run for re-election in order to focus on the pro-slavery migration into Kansas. His colorful oratory gained him a reputation as a loud and passionate speaker "aggressive, explosive, and sometimes wild-eyed when handing an issue that he held dear."[9] Atchison wrote to Amos A. Lawrence, treasurer of the New England Emigrant Aid Society, that "I and my friends wish to make Kansas in all respects like Missouri. Our interests require it. Our peace through all time demands it, and we intend to leave nothing undone that will conduce to that end."[10] He actively recruited groups of men, called blue lodges, to counter the voice of the abolitionists. In spring of 1855, 5,000 armed men from Missouri crossed the border into Kansas to vote in the election of the territorial legislature. (Any man with a "claim" to land in Kansas could vote.) Atchison encouraged them to go to the polls to intimidate the Free Soilers, but he did not go over the border himself.

Doniphan supported popular sovereignty at first, seeing it as a means to stem the growing power of abolitionists. He got caught up in the hysteria over the border conflict and assisted Atchison in recruiting men to march into Kansas to vote for expanding slavery. Atchison's passion for the expansion of slavery, aided by his inflammatory rhetoric and militant actions, continued unabated. He participated in a subsequent raid on Lawrence in 1856 where he made a half dozen speeches on horseback, riding between different companies.[11] Doniphan, however, stopped short of going along on the Lawrence raid. Although he supported pro-slavery migration to Kansas, Doniphan hoped that efforts would remain nonviolent and within the bounds of the law. His efforts thereafter centered on finding a peaceful solution to the popular sovereignty problem, becoming director of the Clay County Pro-Slavery Aid Association to raise money to support those wishing to emigrate to Kansas.

The institution of slavery was imbedded in the culture in which Doniphan and Atchison were raised. The issue was a hot topic the Founding Fathers grappled with, and Congress attempted to resolve without success over the years. Those opposing slavery cited it as a moral issue about the treatment of their fellow man, appealing to a natural law beyond the status quo set by the U.S. Constitution at the time. But slavery was proving economically useful to others, particularly in the South. Doniphan's family engaged in farming during his youth with the help of eighteen slaves. Upon his father's death, he inherited one slave from his father's estate and would own a total of five slaves in 1860.[12] Slavery was an acceptable means of supporting commerce in the view of many Southerners. Doniphan viewed slaves as chattel subject to the property rights and legal protections guaranteed by the law for all property. Doniphan envisioned the eventual abolition of slavery but opposed a sudden end to the institution as being too harsh a change for the southern economy to survive.[13] He honored the legal rules that guided the status of free and enslaved individuals, representing slaves in several cases to enforce their legal entitlement to manumission.

Atchison had similar views on slavery but did not bow to the inevitability of the elimination of it. He owned sixteen slaves to farm his land in Clinton County in 1860.[14] The necessity of agricultural labor was the impetus behind the politics of popular sovereignty, which Atchison intended to use to garner votes for expansion of slaveholding territory. He asserted that because slaves were property, citizens had a right to defend their property, which could not be taken from them without due process of law.[15] By 1858, the polarization of the political situation was intensifying. Abraham Lincoln gave his speech declaring that "a house divided against itself cannot stand," which brought him national prominence. The pro-slavery movement became more convinced that secession was inevitable. Attempts by Northerners to limit slavery would be a major factor in Atchison's decision to support the secession of Missouri from the U.S.

Doniphan remained sympathetic to the concerns of the southern states, but also valued survival of the Union. He had ancestors who fought in the Revolutionary War, regularly emphasizing during his speeches the sacrifices and patriotism that brought the Union into being. Doniphan actively supported John Bell of Tennessee for President in the 1860 election. In his opinion, Bell was the only candidate likely to prevent dissolution of the Union by appealing to moderate voters and preventing extremists at either end of the political spectrum from taking over the executive branch of government. Doniphan traveled the countryside urging others to seek peace through moderation. The election of Lincoln, he argued, would lead to inevitable strife and border warfare. On the day before the national election, he spoke for three hours to a gathering in the upper courtroom in Liberty, stressing that the U.S. Constitution ensured both majority rule and protection of minority rights.[16]

The desire of a substantial number of residents to remain neutral, plus admiration for Doniphan's arguments, convinced many to vote for Bell, who carried Clay County. Abraham Lincoln did not receive even one vote in Clay County, even though he had a relative practicing law in Liberty. National elections results, however, favored Lincoln. The three other presidential candidates received almost a million votes more than Lincoln, but as they were split between the three of them, Lincoln carried the election with less than the popular vote, the first president of the U.S. to do so. Lincoln's election was the realization of Doniphan's worst fears. Abolitionists gained a controlling foothold in the federal government. Pro-slavery proponents began campaigning in earnest for secession.

Most of the population was willing to watch and wait at first, with a few vocal extremist voices on each side. Henry Routt and Judge J.T.V. Thompson warned in a public meeting on December 24, 1860 that the citizens should prepare for action but did not state when this might happen. The *Liberty Tribune* editor, Robert Miller, expressed hope that Lincoln would be constrained from interfering with the South since Congress and the Supreme Court were not of the same mind.[17] Another countywide meeting was held at the courthouse in Liberty on January 28, 1861. Over two thousand residents attended, overflowing from the courthouse and filling the yard outside. Doniphan delivered a ninety-minute speech pleading with residents to remain in the Union and seek compromise.

Doniphan had been impressed by the efforts of Senator John J. Crittenden of Kentucky to find a compromise that would resolve the impending crisis. Crittenden's committee of thirteen senators proposed a series of amendments to the U.S. Constitution that would insure the permanence of slavery states where it already existed, prohibit slavery in new territories, prohibit the abolition of slavery on federal property unless the state in which it was located agreed, and impose federal regulation of internal slave trade and the handling of fugitive slaves. The Crittenden Resolution was approved at the Liberty meeting with "19 [of] 20 of the crowd by holding up hands" in support, according to Doniphan.[18]

Doniphan was selected to attend several conferences in an attempt to keep Missouri in the Union. With Elijah Norton and James H. Moss, he attended a State Convention in St. Louis with instructions to oppose secession. At this point, former Governor Sterling Price concurred with remaining in the Union. Doniphan also attended a Peace Conference in Washington D.C. in February 1861 to promote the Crittenden Resolution as the formula for peace. Representatives delivered stump speeches that reinforced their positions with little movement toward compromise. As a result, nothing was resolved. It was during the convention in Washington that Doniphan met Lincoln in person. He wrote to his nephew that Lincoln was "a man of no intelligence, no enlargement of views [an] easily flattered into a belief that he is King Canute and can say to the waves of revolution 'no further.' The consequence is [that he] is, for the time being, the arbiter of the destinies of this mighty nation [and] if rash, may at any time ruin all beyond redemption." Discouraged, he shared his concern that Missouri should not leave the Union before other states. "One respectable republic in numbers and power is better than twenty little rickety concerns," but that going with the South would be best.[19]

Doniphan soon thought better of this and resumed his efforts to keep Missouri in the Union. Reporting in a meeting of the Missouri General Assembly in St. Louis in March 1861, he stated that the only way to preserve the government was to remove the slavery issue from politics: "I am a Union Man. I go for the whole Union. I live by hope and as a Union man I shall only die when that hope dies."[20] Doniphan returned to western Missouri, speaking at local rallies, appealing to the patriotism of his listeners to preserve the Constitution and the blessings of democracy.

Then matters turned for the worse when Fort Sumner fell into secessionist hands on April 12, 1861. Ten days later, a group of Clay County men took control of the U.S. military arsenal overlooking the Missouri River south of Liberty and removed the armaments stored there, to be placed in hands of the secessionists. Liberty lawyer Henry Routt was one of the leaders of the group. This alerted federal forces, who promptly seized the state militia's camp in St. Louis. Former Governor Sterling Price was outraged by this act of war against his state and threw in with the secessionists. He was appointed by pro-secessionist Governor Claiborne Fox Jackson to lead the Missouri State Guard.

Atchison now publicly supported secession. He accepted an appointment as General in the Missouri State Guard and actively recruited men in northern Missouri. In July 1861, he accompanied Governor Jackson to Richmond, Virginia, to visit his old law school friend Jefferson Davis, to seek aid for Missouri. This resulted in a pledge of $1,000,000 in aid for use of Missouri troops cooperating with the Confederate Army. Atchison counseled Governor Jackson on the procedures for ratification of the government-in-exile's alliance with the Confederacy. Atchison became involved in the Battle of Blue Mills Landing near Liberty while delivering a message to secessionist troops to join General Price at Lexington. He was with Governor Jackson as they fled Jefferson City in advance of federal troops. In August 1861, Atchison fought with Price's troops at Wilson's Creek near Springfield, Missouri and the Battle of Elk Horn in Arkansas.

Defeat by federal forces convinced Atchison to leave for Texas, where he remained for the rest of the war.[21]

Doniphan was also incensed by the entry of federal troops into the state, but still hoped for peace. On April 26, 1861, he spoke at a rally in Platte County and another in Liberty, urging the preservation of the Constitution through compromise. His increasingly fervent speeches in favor of continued loyalty to the Union appealed to fewer and fewer listeners. Doniphan's insistence on personal neutrality also created ill will. His stellar military record made him an ideal candidate to command troops fighting for the southern cause, but in May 1861, he turned down an offer by Governor Jackson to place him in command of the Fifth Division of the Missouri State Guard, citing poor health.

Secessionists were disappointed that the hero of the Mexican War refused command of state troops forming to repel the anticipated federal invasion. They were not impressed by his declaration that he could not raise his hand against the American flag he fought for, as a good number of the men he fought with did just that. Doniphan tried to explain his decision to friends at Liberty Christian Church at the end of the war, stating that his Christian beliefs were first and foremost in his decision not to rebel[22] or fight his friends who did rebel. Doniphan's insistence on compromise rather than submission, however, did not translate into acceptance by those strictly loyal to the Union either. His brother-in-law John C.C. Thornton became a Lieutenant in the Confederate Army, raising Unionists' suspicion by association.

Doniphan continued to make appeals for peace. In June 1861, he wrote to his nephew about the state of local sentiments. Doniphan stated intentions and actions differed, wryly mentioning the "agitation of some valiant gentlemen who paid a short visit to the arsenal not long since. They do not feel much confidence in the pacific disposition of [Union General] Lyon ... I hope we will get on quietly as the secessionists now insist they can do nothing by themselves ... although they are nearly spoiling inwardly for a fight with Lincoln, Blair & Co."[23]

Doniphan attended a convention in Jefferson City in July 1861 to select a replacement for Governor Jackson. Hamilton R. Gamble, a Unionist, was selected. His committee proposed that an explicit declaration be made that there was no adequate cause of Missouri to leave the Union and to oppose the use of force by either the federal government or seceding states. Robert Miller, editor of The Liberty Tribune, who had previously aligned the newspaper's editorial views with Doniphan's political views, started to sour on loyalty to the Union. The masthead of the paper was changed from "The Union, The Constitution, and the Enforcement of the Laws" after the August 9, 1861 edition. The new masthead, "Devoted to Politics, Markets, and General News," was more conducive to ongoing business.

Military defeats at Lexington and Wilson's Creek dimmed the hopes for a quick end to the war and for preservation of Southern sentiments. Henry Routt was arrested and convicted of treason in St. Louis. James Lincoln, another Liberty lawyer who was related to the President, interceded and obtained a pardon for Routt. Doniphan began urging residents to voluntarily take an oath of loyalty to the Union. At a rally in Liberty in April 1862, he argued that secession by Missouri was a delusion. Henry Routt, among others, thought better of defying federal authorities and took the loyalty oath and lived quietly for the remainder of the war.

Doniphan foresaw an economic downturn as soon after hostilities began. On the day Fort Sumter was captured, he wrote to his nephew that "everything here is awful – no money – nothing sells, nothing doing, nothing to see – nothing to do.[24] Liberty merchants informed customers in their ads that due to "the pestilence of war, goods cannot be purchased in the East or in St. Louis for anything but money or its equivalent." Merchants adopted a cash only policy to weather the storm.[25] By October 1863 notices of sheriff's sales of real estate for unpaid taxes filled half The Liberty Tribune. The editor of the Tribune announced that, "we have examined the Delinquent Tax list for Clay County, and the size of it is enormous—embracing the names of hundreds of the wealthiest and staunchest citizens of the county."[26]

The likelihood of lost fortunes and social standing prompted violent reactions in western Missouri. Counties with high default rates on debt had twice as many "bushwhackers" incidents. Many young men of fighting age joined in guerilla warfare to defend their way of life or to disrupt the forces they saw as opposing their way of life. Killings, thefts, and property destruction were common, and many people left the county.[27] Between 1863 and 1864, the violence even disrupted the judicial system. Twenty-one Missouri courthouses were burned during the war. The October 1864 term of court in Clay County was cancelled. Union men also victimized residents. Atchison's sister-in-law was the victim of an attack by Union sympathizers who came to the family farm demanding weapons. Margaret Atchison was hung by her neck while interrogated but managed to survive the assault.[28]

After Quantrill's raid on Lawrence, residents of Clay and Platte Counties became anxious that the Kansas militia would cross the Missouri River to retaliate. Many of the bushwhackers and guerillas were from Clay County. Colonel James H. Moss, leader of the 82nd Regiment of Enrolled Missouri Militia, estimated that 80 percent of the outlaws were Southern sympathizers.[29]

Doniphan, like Atchison earlier, decided to leave the area. His financial situation was also declining. His property had lost significant value due to guerilla activity, and much of his clientele no longer engaged him for legal matters due to suspicions about his true loyalties. On appointment by the governor, he moved to St. Louis where he worked part time as a special claims agent for widows, orphans, and disabled soldiers seeking compensation from the state. He formed a new law firm with William S. Field, a displaced lawyer from Lafayette County with Union leanings. The investments he had made earlier in life in land, banking, and loans to friends rendered Doniphan short of cash. As the war progressed, he was forced to mortgage most of his investments, and then to sell them at a great loss. Other property was foreclosed by Clay County for unpaid taxes. His experience during the war made him skeptical of the ability of government to better the public welfare as well as bitter about future prospects.

Atchison assessed the political climate before returning to Missouri following the war, finally deciding that he would be better off in Missouri, which did not leave the Union, than in Texas, where secession meant domination under reconstruction. He wrote to Margaret in August 1865 that he would return the following spring, but he was still concerned. "I have much to write but scared to do it. I know not whose hands my letters may fall into."[30] Atchison returned to live on his Clinton County farm near Gower.

Doniphan and Atchison's views continued along separate paths following the war. Doniphan eventually returned to western Missouri where he engaged in banking and the practice of law in Richmond.

Atchison kept a low profile for the rest of his life, perhaps having learned that the federal government could exact substantial retribution. In his view of affairs, "all departments of government are corrupt and rotten. The people are demoralized to an extent little short of Sodom and Gomorrah."[31] The people of Clay County were demoralized too. Attempts were made to heal the wounds of division, but there was no attempt to raise the American flag over the Clay County courthouse again until 1912.

Endnotes

1. Roger D. Launius, *Alexander William Doniphan: Portrait of a Missouri Moderate*, (Columbia: University of Missouri Press (1997).

2. William E. Parrish, *David Rice Atchison of Missouri, Border Politician, in University of Missouri Studies Vol. XXXIV, No. 1*, (Columbia: University of Missouri Press, 1961).

3. Parrish, *Border Politician*, William E. Parrish, 7.

4. Launius, *Portrait of a Missouri Moderate*, 4.

5. Gov. Boggs, Executive Order 44 (1838), Archives of Missouri Secretary of State. This order as rescinded by Gov. Christopher S. Bond on June 25, 1976.

6. W.H. Woodson, *History of Clay & Platte County*, 38-42; W.H. Woodson, History of Clay County, Missouri, (Topeka & Indianapolis: Historical Publishing Company, 1920), 113.

7. *The Plattsburg Lever*, "Gen. D.R. Atchison: Chat with a Man Who was President of the Unites States for Thirty-six Hours," September 8, 1882, in possession of the Clinton County Historical Society.

8. P.L. Gray, *Doniphan County History*, (Bendina, KS: Roycroft Press, 1905), 12.

9. *New York Tribune*, October 10, 1854.

10. Parrish, *Border Politician*, 165, 178.

11. Parrish, *Border Politician*, 200-201. Atchison was known to get excited and say more than he intended in public speeches. He claimed his intent on this occasion was to speak "in the interest of peace, exerting myself to check, not to incite, outrage." Unfortunately, the forces of destruction had already been set in motion and a hotel and several other business establishments were destroyed.

12. 1860 Slave Schedule, 1860 U.S. Federal Census for Clay County, MO.

13. Doniphan attended a convention called by the Missouri Governor toward the end of the Civil War to determine the method for freeing slaves in Missouri. Doniphan supported a bill granting limited emancipation on July 4, 1870 for slaves over age forty. Slaves under age twelve were to be kept in servitude until age twenty-three (as late as 1892) and those between twelve and forty would be freed on July 4, 1876.

14. 1860 Slave Schedule, 1860 U.S. Federal Census for Clinton County, MO. Atchison felt responsible for the future welfare of his slaves at the end of the war. He wrote to his brother in August 1865: "[I] must take the best care of them I can, if I leave them God only knows what would become of them ... Negroes are now worth less than nothing; everybody is trying to get rid of them upon almost any terms."

15. This was the argument successfully made by the owner of Dred Scott, a Missouri slave, before the U.S. Supreme Court a few years later. This was conclusion of the ruling by Chief Justice Roger Taney that negroes, whether slaves or free, were not accorded citizenship rights under the U.S. Constitution. *Dred Scott v. Sandford,* 60 U.S. 393 (1857).

16. *The Liberty Tribune* reported on Doniphan's speaking engagements in Independence, Liberty, Lexington, Missouri City, and Platte City. They were "replete with sound political wisdom and experience." *The Liberty Tribune,* August 3, 24, and 31, 1860; September 14 and 28, 1860; and November 9, 1860. Clay County Archives and Historical Museum newspaper collection.

17. W.H. Woodson, *History of Clay County, Missouri,* (Liberty: Clay County Archives and Historical Library, 2016 reprint of 1885 edition), 187-188.

18. Alexander Doniphan, letter to John Doniphan, January 28, 1861. The State Historical Society of Missouri, Doniphan Letters, Collection file C-29. John Doniphan, a nephew, was a lawyer in Weston, Platte County.

19. Alexander Doniphan, letter to John Doniphan, February 22, 1861. The State Historical Society of Missouri, Doniphan Letters, Collection file C-29.

20. Launius, *Portrait of a Missouri Moderate,* 251.

21. Sarah Smith, "A Civil War Incident at Atchison Farm," Collection of the Clinton County Historical Society.

22. Alexander Doniphan, letter to D.C. Allen, February 3, 1865,

23. Alexander Doniphan, letter to John Doniphan, June 3, 1861. The State Historical Society of Missouri, Doniphan Letters, Collection file C-29.

24. Alexander Doniphan, letter to John Doniphan, April 12, 1861. The State Historical Society of Missouri, Doniphan Letters, Collection file C-29.

25. *The Liberty Tribune,* June 3, 1861 and April 11, 1862. Newspaper Collection of the Clay County Archives and Historical Library.

26. *The Liberty Tribune,* November 13, 1863. Newspaper Collection of the Clay County Archives and Historical Library.

27. Woodson, *History of Clay County,* 247.

28. Sarah Smith, "A Civil War Incident at Atchison Farm," Collection of the Clinton County Historical Society.

29. Woodson, *History of Clay County*, 241.

30. David Rice Atchison, letter to Margaret B. Atchison and Wm. Atchison Esq., August 12, 1865, Collection of Clinton County Historical Society.

31. Parrish, *Border Politician*, 223.

CHAPTER 9

Mr. Doniphan Goes to Court

J. Bradley Pace

Starting with observations on his statue in front of the Ray County Courthouse, this article focuses on nineteenth century courthouses, many of which Doniphan would have practiced within.

Chapter Page Image: Alexander W. Doniphan statue in front of the Ray County Courthouse in Richmond, MO. *-- Anderson, Valerie. (2020, April 29). Doniphan Statue at the Ray County Courthouse [Photograph]. Giving River Images, Richmond, MO.*

Ray County Courthouse, completed 1914, with Doniphan statue in foreground. Courthousehistory.com

Some years ago, as a newly minted young lawyer, I traveled to Richmond, Missouri for a court appearance. Arriving a bit early, I took the opportunity to look around the courthouse grounds. I quickly came across an impressive larger-than-life statue of Alexander William Doniphan. I was vaguely aware he had been a lawyer and military figure, but that was about it. So, I stopped to read the inscriptions found on the brass plaques at the base of the statue:

> Front plaque
>
> In honor of Alexander W. Doniphan. Commander of First Regiment Missouri Mounted Volunteers. Born Mason County, Kentucky, July 9, 1808. Died Richmond, Missouri, August 8, 1887. On the roster of the great soldiers of the earth must always stand in a halo of glory the name of Colonel Alexander W. Doniphan of Missouri.

Rear plaque

Colonel Doniphan was of immense stature, noble appearance, brilliant parts, fearless, of great moral courage, sanguine, faithful, just, poetic in temperament, the champion of the downtrodden, eloquent beyond description, and without doubt entitled to be classed among the greatest orators and lawyers that ever lived.

Even allowing for the flattery sometimes found on statues, the inscriptions are an amazing tribute. I felt the urge to learn more about any man who could garner such praise. I would have been even more impressed had I known that over 20,000 people gathered on the Richmond square in 1918 for the unveiling of his state-commissioned statue.[1]

Doniphan's state-comissioned statue was unveiled in 1918.

It is daunting to approach the study of a life as rich as Doniphan's. Much has been written, with more to follow. There are, of course, numerous archives and museums with artifacts to help us understand his accomplishments. These are essential, but we can also learn from some relics not found in museums. Scattered across Missouri, in town squares from the Ozarks to the banks of the Mississippi, are nineteenth century county courthouses we can visit today. These structures were built during Doniphan's legal career, yet have survived to become a part of our modern world. They are a tangible link to Missouri's past. After well over one hundred years of service, each surviving building has a story to tell.

After studying law for two years, Doniphan was admitted to the Kentucky bar in 1829, at the tender age of twenty-one. The following year he headed west to Missouri to seek his fortune in the law.[2] He would practice law in Missouri for the remainder of his life. He first settled in Lexington, before moving on to Liberty just three years later.[3] In 1846, Doniphan answered the call of duty and joined the First Missouri Mounted Volunteer Regiment, leading their legendary expedition to Mexico.[4] In 1847, he returned to Liberty to resume his law practice. There he continued to hone his legendary talents for oratory. The outbreak of the Civil War in 1861 caused Doniphan to relocate to St. Louis.[5] Following the war, he moved again, this time setting up practice in Richmond, where he remained until his death in 1887.[6]

Over the course of his long career as a prominent Missouri lawyer, Doniphan would have appeared in courtrooms all across the state. Lawyers in his day would sometimes follow a judge around a judicial circuit, which would typically involve several counties. Although known as a defense lawyer,[7] most nineteenth century lawyers would have, for reasons of economic necessity, handled a variety of cases—from a contract dispute on one day,

The Clay County Courthouse in 1857, which was demolished in 1934.

to a will or criminal matter the next. During his forty-six years of practice, Doniphan would have become a familiar courthouse figure.

The county courthouses in which Doniphan appeared were designed and built with pride. In the age before the automobile, people spent most of their lives within the confines of their county limits. A grand courthouse was proof of the greatness of the county, and a source of satisfaction for civic boosters. A courthouse might include elaborate ornamentation, or classical Romanesque or Greek design elements. Often they were topped with a large dome or costly clock tower. When first constructed, many were the most architecturally significant buildings in their county, and some remain so still.

Cities and towns competed vigorously for the coveted status of county seat. County government, traditionally housed in the courthouse, included school boards, tax commissions, roads, and other public offices. Legal actions, both large and small, would play out daily in the courthouse. All this additional traffic meant a bustling and prosperous town square, with the courthouse located right at the center. Communities were literally and figuratively built around their courthouses. Although somewhat diminished by today's interstate highways, county seats historically served as market centers and transportation hubs.

The courthouses in which Doniphan appeared most often would have been in Clay County (Liberty), and Ray County (Richmond). Unfortunately, both of these structures were demolished and replaced long ago. The courthouse in Liberty stood from 1857 to 1934.[8] The Richmond Courthouse lasted even longer. The temple design of the Richmond Courthouse, similar in appearance to the courthouse in Lafayette County, opened in 1856. It was used by the court until 1914, when it was purchased by the United Mine Workers. They then proceeded to move the entire structure to make way for the new courthouse. The 1856 courthouse lasted until it fell into disrepair and was finally razed in the 1960s.[9] While these historic buildings are lost, we can still see and visit other nineteenth century courthouses where Doniphan could have appeared.

Doniphan would almost certainly have appeared on behalf of clients in nearby Lafayette County, named for Revolutionary War hero General Lafayette. Its courthouse was erected in 1847,[10] and sits at the center of the charming town of Lexington. A fine example of pre–Civil War architecture, it features four massive sandstone, Ionic unfluted columns said to have been produced in a quarry near Warrensburg.[11] Originally the courthouse cupola did not include a clock, which was added in 1886. Its interior boasts pressed tin ceilings and paintings of early Lafayette County.[12]

Doniphan would recognize the building's most celebrated feature—a cannon ball embedded in the east column. The ball, now held in place with an iron rod, is said to have struck the column during the siege and Battle of Lexington, September 18 to 21, 1861.[13] During the battle, Confederate General Sterling W. Price defeated the Union forces under Colonel J. A. Mulligan. Prior to the battle, Union troops occupied Lexington and prevented Missouri State Guard forces north and south of the Missouri River from uniting. The Confederate victory broke the Union barricade.[14] As a strong Unionist, Doniphan would have followed news of this battle closely, and mourned the result.

Today a plaque on the Lafayette County Courthouse heralds it to be the oldest in continuous use west of the Mississippi! Residents of Jackson County may take some exception to this claim since the Independence Courthouse was completed a few years earlier in 1838,[15] based on a foundation laid ten years earlier.[16] The Jackson County Courthouse has been substantially remodeled and expanded multiple times. During its major 1933 remodeling, overseen by Presiding Judge Harry Truman, court sessions were temporarily relocated to the 1827 log courthouse.[17] This pause gives rise to the claim by Lafayette County as the oldest courthouse in continuous use. No doubt Colonel Doniphan would be impressed with the appearance of the Jackson County Courthouse today, with its 1933 remodeling inspired by Independence Hall in Philadelphia. Although he would not recognize the building now, parts of the original structure are still visible in the second-floor courtroom and in the attic.[18]

During the Civil War, Clay County held definite Southern sympathies. With his strong Unionist leanings, Doniphan was likely at odds with many of his neighbors and clients.[19] This would have influenced his decision to relocate to St. Louis in 1862, where he found work as a lawyer with the Missouri Claims Commission dealing with pension claims for war refugees.[20] It is likely he had occasion to appear in the St. Louis County Courthouse, the grandest ever built in Missouri. This cruciform, Greek Revival–style building was constructed around an existing 1828 Federal-style courthouse, and was completed in sections from 1839 to 1862.[21] Its massive 128 ton cast-iron dome was the last major construction phase, from 1860 to 1861. This Italian Renaissance dome was modeled after St. Peter's Basilica in Rome. Sturdy cast-iron stairways in use for well over a century can be found throughout the courthouse. For all its extravagance, the building's most novel feature may have been its public restrooms, said to be the first ones west of the Mississippi.[22]

During its years as the seat of justice for St. Louis County, a wide range of landmark events occurred within the courthouse's limestone walls. It played a key role in the escalation of tensions between the North and South when in 1847 and 1850, Dred Scott sued for his freedom from slavery.[23] When the decision against Scott was upheld by the US Supreme Court in 1857, abolitionists and states' rights advocates were irretrievably polarized. Doniphan would have closely followed this court case since although he strongly supported the Union, he was also a slave owner.[24] Two years later, St. Louis area resident Ulysses S. Grant appeared at the courthouse to legally free his only slave. Slave auctions, however, continued to be held on the courthouse steps until 1861. These sales occurred as part of the settlement process for probate estates.[25] Another early civil rights event occurred at the St. Louis courthouse when in 1872, it was the site of suffragist Virginia Louisa Minor's unsuccessful voting rights suit.[26] Today known as the "Old St. Louis Courthouse," it is part of the

Gateway Arch National Park, and is operated by the National Park Service.

The next courthouse on our state-wide tour is in New London, Ralls County, north from St. Louis. This structure was completed in 1858,[27] and features a Greek Revival–style façade with a four columned front portico. Today it appears much as it did in Doniphan's time. Its second-floor courtroom is well known among Missouri lawyers for its superior acoustics. This Stradivarius of courtrooms would have suited Doniphan's legendary talent for oratory. Lacking modern technology, its fine acoustical quality is achieved by insulating the courtroom walls with sawdust, with the back wall being curved.[28] This arrangement would have perfectly captured the rich timbre and pitch of Doniphan's strong voice.

1868 Moniteau County Courthouse.

If Doniphan ever made a court appearance in Moniteau County, California, Missouri, he would have been impressed with the building's symmetry. Its design follows the classic revival–style, and is influenced by the Missouri state capital building.[29] The front façade features a two-story semi-circular portico, with two full brick columns and two half columns, all round and in Corinthian style. White pine woodwork and 24-paned windows add to the overall elegant appearance. Residents of Moniteau County (derived from the French spelling of the Algonquin Indian word, manito, meaning spirit) were rightfully proud of this structure when it was completed in 1868. To celebrate, they held a grand ball in the courtroom.[30] Decades later, the party was still news when in 1937 the California Democrat, described the ball as a county social event without peer. Presumably invitations were sent far and wide, with the attendees being a who's who in the state. Each male attendant paid $2.50 which entitled him and a female guest to four regular meals and the ball supper. On the first day of festivities, partygoers began to arrive by foot or horseback around noon. Immediately after lunch, the ball officially opened. It is reported to have continued unabated for the next twenty-four hours. Dancing and merrymaking were the order of the day, and night! The courtroom hosted, at alternate times up, to twenty-four couples dancing the cotillion, or three double lines for the Virginia reel. We will never know if the revelers included Doniphan, but his celebrity status certainly warranted an invite.

Today a courthouse might seem a bizarre place to hold a ball, but Moniteau County was not alone in this practice. When the Platte County Courthouse in Platte City was completed in 1867, a Valentine's Day ball featuring a dance and carousel was held in the courtroom.[31] At this time, Doniphan was living in the not-too-distant Richmond. As a prominent and socially active Missouri lawyer, he certainly could have been invited. His high regard would have ensured a full dance card!

The attention paid to a new courthouse reflected their importance in nineteenth century life. When in 1873, St. Joseph in Buchanan County held cornerstone ceremonies for its new courthouse, the festivities featured speakers and a large parade with a brass band. Numerous items were sealed in the cornerstone, including newspapers, coins, and photographs. Thousands of onlookers listened patiently through many speeches. The master of ceremonies announced to the crowd that the courthouse should promote harmony and brotherly love. Colonel John Doniphan (no relation to Alexander W. Doniphan), elaborated that it should be a place where the scales of justice would be evenly held.[32]

At the time of its construction, the Buchanan County Courthouse was the largest in the state outside St. Louis, with a center dome rising 145 feet from ground level. Its rich history includes the arraignment and sentencing of the Ford brothers, who killed Jesse James.[33] Tempted by a $10,000 reward offered by the express and railroad companies, and the State's promise of immunity, Charley and Bob Ford shot and killed Jesse in St. Joseph on April 3, 1882. James had been living in St. Joseph since 1881. Unfortunately for the Ford brothers, the prosecuting attorney for Buchanan County insisted on prosecuting them. At the arraignment, the Fords pled guilty. Both were sentenced to be hanged. One month prior to their execution, Governor Crittenden pardoned the two men, who were eventually able to collect their reward money. As a man of the law, Doniphan must have viewed with concern this messy chronology of events. Ironically, controversy still exists as to the true identity of the individual killed by the Fords that day in 1882.

The cornerstone ceremony held on October 8, 1888 for the new Barton County Courthouse in Lamar was a countywide celebration. Events included a parade headed by the Lamar Band, followed by the Masonic order, and area schools. The parade marched around the town square before entering a park where the official program began. Among the items sealed in the cornerstone include corn, wine, oil, coins, newspapers, the Holy Bible, and a copy of the constitution.[34]

A good example of a building commissioned to achieve more than mere functionality is the courthouse in Maryville, Nodaway County. Completed in 1882, it was designed by the prominent architect and French native Edmond Eckel, a graduate of the Ecole des Beaux Arts in Paris.[35] It features Romanesque motifs, ornamental stonework, and an elegant clocktower reaching 140 feet high, which still impresses after over a hundred years and counting.

A courthouse clocktower was a coveted feature on any nineteenth century town square. As a successful lawyer, Alexander W. Doniphan could afford his own pocket watch, but for many people an expensive timepiece was beyond reach. The chiming of a town clock was not just for the charm—it was a practical way for people on the square to keep time. It was also a high-tech status symbol that proclaimed the wealth and success of the county.

When the 1859 Miller County Courthouse in Tuscumbia was remodeled in 1910, no money was available for a costly clock in the tower. This Ozark-area county hoped the necessary funds would eventually be raised. In the meantime, a temporary illusion was created by simply painting a clockface in the tower, set at eight o'clock on all four sides. The tower has been repainted many times over the decades, and each time the "clocks which never ran" are renewed.[36] The court moved out of this building in 2002. It is now in the hands of a private owner with possible plans for use as a bed and breakfast.

Just prior to the outbreak of the Civil War, Cass County purchased bricks for a new courthouse in Harrisonville.[37] This inopportune timing forced the county to drop its plans and sell the 300,000 unused bricks. Cass County would not complete its new courthouse until 1897, and then its tower was missing a clock. Insufficient funds were the culprit. Fortunately, a grass roots citizens group came to the rescue. So it was that on May 11, 1908, the Harrisonville Town Clock Club was organized.[38] This all female group met regularly in the courthouse ladies' lounge, then called the "Ladies Rest Room." This club organized all manner of fundraising events, including pie suppers, a laziest man contest, most industrious woman contest, and a female minstrel show. Including the $200 donated by the county court, the necessary $1,231 was raised within one year. The timepiece which was eventually installed boasts a 1,200 pound bell, 12 gross of screws, and 10 pounds of nails. The four dials for this impressive clock each required 250 feet of white pine lumber. By the twenty-first century, most counties had replaced their high maintenance mechanical clock workings with cheaper electric motors. In 2015, Cass County opted to repair its original clock. A state historic preservation grant covered 70 percent of the $106,450 cost.[39]

Like Cass County, the 1887 Howard County Courthouse in Fayette, also included a "lounge" complete with comfortable furnishings and even a piano. This room was used for decades as a social gathering place, and by town square shoppers or weary travelers just needing a place to rest.[40] Obsolete today, but a real community asset in Doniphan's time.

Iron County erected its one and only courthouse in 1858, for the sum of approximately $14,000. Constructed largely of handmade red brick, it reflects both Greek Revival and Italian architectural elements, a combination termed Italianate Classicism. A gazebo-like bandstand added in 1899 features fanciful gingerbread ornamentation and cut-out designs in the form of stars and crescents.[41] Like similar bandstands on small town squares, this little structure has long been a community focal point for concerts, speeches, civic events, and even Christmas caroling.

The Iron County Courthouse in Ironton played a central role in the Battle of Pilot Knob, on September 27, 1864.[42] Confederate Major General Sterling W. Price, of Battle of Lexington fame, led a motley expedition up from Arkansas into Missouri, with the ultimate aim of St. Louis. Word of Union troops in St. Louis caused Price to divert to Pilot Knob. Eventually, Confederate and Union troops met in bloody fighting in Iron County. Skirmishing near the courthouse left cannon and rifle scars, which can still be seen today. During the battle, the courthouse served as barracks and was occupied at alternate times by Confederate and Union troops. After the fighting, which was a Union victory, it was pressed into duty as a badly needed hospital.

The Macon County courthouse also has Civil War roots. The county seat at the start of the war was Bloomington, home to many Southern sympathizers. Seen as a military threat, Union General Lewis Merrill ordered Major Thomas Moody to burn Bloomington to the ground.[43] Perhaps mindful of his place in history, Major Moody was reluctant to follow such a harsh order.

As a compromise, Moody was allowed to run for the state legislature with the promise to introduce a bill to move the county seat from Bloomington to Macon as an "act of military necessity."[44] Moody was elected, and thus Macon, then a strategic railroad junction, became the new seat of justice for Macon County. Major Moody could have been influenced by Alexander W. Doniphan's famous refusal to follow another harsh order, when as a Brigadier General in 1838, Doniphan refused an order by General Samuel D. Lucas of the State Militia to execute Joseph Smith Jr., founder of The Church of Jesus Christ of Latter-day Saints.[45]

The courthouse in the new seat of Macon was completed in 1865, and is still in use today. In an appearance unusual for a Missouri courthouse, it features fenestration and an ornate cornice design repeated above the recessed double front doors. Originally, the building was topped with an ornate cupola and clock tower which were removed during renovations in 1940.[46]

In 1875, Lewis County commissioned a small two-story red brick courthouse in Monticello which is still in use today. Located in northeast Missouri, the little town of Monticello prospered as a provider of supplies for area settlers. As can also be seen below, it also drew strength and aspiration from its role as the county seat.

> Here were the lawyers, the politicians, the 'leading men,' and here too, was plenty of whisky, strong and cheap. The old taverns, with all their good cheer, plenty of well-cooked and toothsome fare, comfortable beds and ample bar-rooms were the scenes of many an hour's revel and happy season in the olden time. When the courts were in session, the best legal minds in the state were wont to

congregate at Pemberton's and other taverns, and pass the time merrily during the hours of recess.[47]

We can't know if Doniphan was one of the "leading men" to ever enjoy the "good cheer" of the old taverns in Monticello, but he would have been familiar with county seat revelry.

Salem, in Dent County, provides a different picture of life on a nineteenth century Missouri town square. Built for the cost of $15,500, its circa 1870, Ozark-region courthouse features a Victorian style mansard roof with dormers and cast-iron cresting.[48] Originally its lawn was fenced with wood posts and whitewashed fence boards, with stiles at each corner. To prevent goats, hogs, cattle, and sheep from milling around on the courthouse grounds, the entry steps to this fence were made of three-quarter-inch iron rods. In 1896, the wood fence was replaced by an iron picket fence which was less successful at keeping out

The final hours of the Warren County Courthouse. -- Missouri Department of Natural Resources, Nick Decker

THE WILL OF MISSOURI: THE LIFE, TIMES, & INFLUENCE OF ALEXANDER WILLIAM DONIPHAN

mules, horses, geese, and other wildlife. The following year a city "stock law" was passed to stop the animals' abuse of the courthouse grounds.⁴⁹

Another county located in the beautiful Missouri Ozark Plateau region, is Carter, which is roughly divided north to south by the Current River. Its remote location means that Doniphan probably never visited the county seat, Van Buren. Had he done so, he would have encountered a simple 40-by-40-foot, two-story courthouse, built of Carter County lumber dressed locally by hand. This 1871 structure was remodeled during the Great Depression, with its exterior being expanded and completely

Clark County Courthouse 1871 - 2011.

covered in native Missouri cobblestones.⁵⁰ No doubt this meant badly needed work for citizens of the county. This unique courthouse still serves today, and bears a plaque reading "Franklin D. Roosevelt, President of the United States, W.P.A. Project No. 168, January 21, 1936."

While there are a surprising number of surviving nineteenth century Missouri courthouses to remind of us of life and times in Doniphan's era, their number continues to dwindle. The plight of the 1872 Warren County courthouse in Warrenton is illustrative. Though placed on the National Register of Historic Places in 1972, it was none the less demolished in 1995. Costs of ongoing maintenance and renovations to meet the Americans with Disabilities Act were deemed prohibitive.⁵¹ Blame for destruction of this grand structure lies not just with the raw economics, but also with a lack of appreciation for the benefits of historic preservation, including heritage tourism.

Another historic Missouri courthouse recently lost was in Kahoka, Clark County, in the extreme northeast corner of the state. This 42-by-72 foot building was completed in 1872.⁵² Until the moment of its demolition in 2011, it provided great insight into 1870s courthouse design. Other than white stucco which had been applied in a 1934 Public Works Administration project, it had not been significantly altered. It is not uncommon for the cupola of an old courthouse to be removed for maintenance reasons, but this one had remained intact. The design for the octagonal-shaped cupola tower did not include a clock. With its original appearance and rural setting, one could imagine lawyers, perhaps even Doniphan himself, arriving for "law day" by horseback or wagon. Preservation groups fought to save the building, arguing that the cost of saving it would not exceed the price of a new building. Unfortunately, this piece of Clark County history was forever lost to the wrecking ball.

Alexander W. Doniphan dedicated his life to the rule of law. He would be pleased to find that so many courthouses from his era have survived. We can only wonder what he might think of today's modern county justice centers, which have traded stylistic design elements for stark efficiency and metal detectors. They clearly have a tough act to follow. But if Doniphan were to enter a Missouri courthouse today, he would see lawyers arguing their cases just as he did over a century ago. The courthouse still embodies those elusive goals of justice and good governance.

The next time you happen to be on a Missouri town square and spot an old courthouse, stop and look around. See it up close for yourself. Read its plaques and inscriptions. Notice its scars. Take a moment to reflect on the likes of Alexander William Doniphan. Listen for the ghosts of the past.

Endnotes

1. Raycountymuseum.angelfire.com/alexander-doniphan.html

2. Alexander William Doniphan, by Judge R. Kenneth Elliott (ret.), published June 22, 2012, Clay County Archives and Historical Library – Liberty, Missouri.

3. Ibid.

4. Alexander W. Doniphan – Winding River History and Natural Resources. Windingriver.com/alexander_w_doniphan

5. Id.

6. Alexander William Doniphan, by Judge R. Kenneth Elliott (ret.), published June 22, 2012, Clay County Archives and Historical Library – Liberty, Missouri

7. Ibid.

8. Marian M. Ohman, "Clay County," Encyclopedia of Missouri Courthouses (Columbia, Missouri: University of Missouri – Columbia Extension Office, 1981), no page number.

9. Id., at Ray County, no page number.

10. "Historic Missouri Courthouses," *Missouri Historical Review* 57, (April 1963), inside back cover.

11. *Lexington Advertiser-News,* March 5, 1962.

12. Informational flier produced by the Lexington Tourism Bureau.

13. Historic Missouri Courthouses," *Missouri Historical Review* 57, (April 1963), inside back cover.

14. Historic markers on the courthouse grounds; William Young, Young's History of Lafayette County, Missouri. Indianapolis: B.F. Bowen and Company, 1919, Vol. I, 60-61.

15. Winding the Clock on the Independence Square, Jackson County's Historic Truman Courthouse, David W. Jackson, Jackson County Historical Society, 2013, 20.

16. Historic marker on courthouse grounds

17. Winding the Clock on the Independence Square, Jackson County's Historic Truman Courthouse, David W. Jackson, Jackson County Historical Society, 2013, 62.

18. Marian M. Ohman, "Jackson County," *Encyclopedia of Missouri Courthouses*, no page number. University of Missouri-Columbia Extension Office, 1981.

19. Alexander William Doniphan, by Judge R. Kenneth Elliott (ret.), published June 22, 2012, Clay County Archives and Historical Library – Liberty, Missouri.

20. Alexander Doniphan – Winding River History and Natural Resources. Windingriver.com/alexander_w_doniphan.

21. Historic Courthouses, *Missouri Historical Review*, 60 (Jan. 1966), back cover; *Time Place*, St. Louis Post-Dispatch Magazine, January 29, 1995.

22. Ibid.; Information sheet prepared by the Jefferson National Expansion Memorial, National Park Service, U.S. Department of the Interior.

23. Ibid.

24. State Historical Society of Missouri, Historic Missourians, Alexander Doniphan, historicmissourians.shsmo.org.

25. Information sheet prepared by the Jefferson National Expansion Memorial, National Park Service, U.S. Department of the Interior.

26. Information sheet prepared by the Jefferson National Expansion Memorial, National Park Service, U.S. Department of the Interior.

27. "Historic Missouri Courthouses," *Missouri Historical Review*, 58 (Jan. 1964), inside back cover.

28. Ibid.; National Register of Historic Places Inventory—Nomination Form, prepared by Sheila M. Hannah, Research Architectural Historian, Missouri State Park Board, State Historical Survey and Planning Office, February 2, 1971.

29. "Historic Missouri Courthouses," *Missouri Historical Review*, 58 (Oct. 1963), inside back cover; Dorothy J. Caldwell, Missouri Historic Sites, Catalogue. Columbia, Missouri: Missouri State Historical Society, 1963; National Register of Historic Places Inventory—Nomination Form. Form prepared by M. Patricia Holmes, Research Architectural Historian, Missouri State Park Board, State Historical Survey and Planning Office, updated.

30. "Grand Inaugural Ball Held for Courthouse 70 Years Ago," *California Democrat*, May 13, 1937.

31. "Historic Missouri Courthouses," *Missouri Historical Review*, 58, (April 1958), inside back cover; National Register of Historic Places—Nomination Form, prepared by Janice R. Cameron, Research Assistant, Department of Natural Resources, Office of Historic Preservation, Jefferson City, Missouri, October 6, 1978.

32. *History of Buchanan County, Missouri, Birdsall, Williams and Company, 1881*, reprinted, Cape Girardeau, Missouri: Ramfre Press, 1974, pp. 338-40.

33. National Register of Historic Places Inventory—Nomination Forms (1972, resubmitted 1978)

34. "County Courthouse Celebrates 100 Years," *The Daily Democrat,* Lamar, Missouri, October 8, 1988.

35. National Register of Historic Places Inventory—Nomination Form, prepared by Thomas W. Carneal, Assistant Professor of History, Northwest Missouri State University, 1980.

36. *Daily Capital News,* Jefferson City, Missouri, May 18, 1960; Ohman, *Encyclopedia of Missouri Courthouses.*

37. Ohman, *Encyclopedia of Missouri Courthouses.*

38. Bulletin of National Association of Watch and Clock Collectors, February 1977.

39. Cass County Democrat Missourian, February 13, 2015.

40. Historic markers on the courthouse grounds; "Battle Won For Historic Courthouse," *Kansas City Times,* January 20, 1970.

41. National Register of Historic Places Inventory—Nomination Form, prepared by Claire F. Blackwell, Arcitectural Historian, Department of Natural Resources, Office of Historic Preservation, Jefferson City, Missouri, 1979.

42. Ibid.; Historic Missouri Courthouses, *Missouri Historical Review,* 58 (July 1964), inside back cover; Cyrus A. Peterson and Joseph Mills Hanson, *Pilot Knob: The Thermopylae of the West,* New York: Neale Publishing Co.

43. National Register of Historic Places Inventory—Nomination Form, prepared by Noelle Soren, Architectural Historian, Office of Historic Preservation, Department of Natural Resources, March 14, 1978.

44. Historic Missouri Courthouses, *Missouri Historical Review,* 59 (July 1965), inside back cover.

45. Judge R. Kenneth Elliott, *Alexander William Doniphan,* by (ret.), published June 22, 2012, Clay County Archives and Historical Library; "Alexander W. Doniphan," WindingRiver, windingriver.com/alexander_w_doniphan.

46. Historic Missouri Courthouses, Missouri Historical Review., Vol. 59 (July 1965), inside back cover; National Register of Historic Places Inventory—Nomination Form, prepared by Noelle Soren, Architectural Historian, Office of Historic Preservation, Department of Natural Resources, March 14, 1978.

47. *History of Lewis, Clark, Knox and Scotland Counties, Missouri.* Chicago: Goodspeed Publishing Company, 1887, Reprinted, Marceline, Missouri: Walswoth Publishing Company, 1981.

48. *Dent County Salem News,* July 11, 1975

49. Ibid., National Register of Historic Places Inventory—Nomination Form, prepared by Sheila M. Hannah, Architectural Historian, Missouri State Park Board, State Historical and Planning Office, May 1, 1971.

50. Gene Oakley, History of Carter County. Van Buren, Missouri: J-G Publications, Missouri 1970; Historic Marker placed by the State Historical Society of Missouri and the State Highway Commission, 1959; Ohman, *Encyclopedia of Missouri Courthouses*.

51. Karen Grace, "Saving Historic Courthouses," *Missouri Resources,* Missouri Department of Natural Resources, 1995; Preservation Issues, Missouri Department of Natural Resources, 6 (5), 2.

52. National Register marker, Ohman, *Encyclopedia of Missouri Courthouses*.

CHAPTER 10

The Trial of His Life

Jeremiah J. Morgan

A fictional account of a trial argued by Doniphan and his law partners.

Chapter Page Image: Compilation of portraits of Alexander Doniphan, Elizabeth Thronton Doniphan, and Alexander Doniphan, Jr. The portrait of Alexander Doniphan has been flipped horizontally to fit into the design aesthetic. -- *Bingham, G. C. (circa 1850.). Portrait of General Alexander William Doniphan [Unsigned oil painting.]. Retrieved July, 2020, from The State Historical Society of Missouri https://digital.shsmo.org/digital/collection/art/id/356/rec/1*

"There are few things in life more precious than life itself ..."

These words ran through Alexander W. Doniphan's mind as he entered the general store Monday morning on November 7, 1847. He had been rehearsing the opening lines of his jury statement for the Harper murder trial set to begin that very day, and these words kept coming to him. But what were those few things more precious than life itself? He was lost in these thought as he pulled the door open.

"Mornin' Colonel Doniphan, what can I do for you?" came the voice of Josiah Stoal, the storekeeper, breaking him out of his reverie.

"Good morning, Josiah," Doniphan responded. "Oh, and please just call me Will."

It had been several months since he returned from the war with Mexico, a war in which he led his men on the longest march in U.S. military history. Along the way, he had even helped write the New Mexico constitution. Missourians had proclaimed him a military hero for his accomplishments. But he was no longer in the military, even if people still insisted on calling him Colonel Doniphan. Now, Will was intent on getting his law practice up and running again. Before heading off to war, he had been a successful lawyer and state legislator, defending some of the most notable citizens of Missouri. He had even defended the Mormon prophet Joseph Smith for several years. It was his law practice, and one of the most important cases of his life, that he was focused on this morning.

"I thought the Harper case started today," said Josiah, emphasizing the very thing Will was thinking about.

"It does, I just thought I would drop off a letter for my son Alexander before heading to the courthouse."

"How's he doing away at school?" asked Josiah.

"Near as I can tell, good," said Will as he handed the letter to the storekeeper. "But it's hard to tell. He doesn't write much."

"Well, I'll make sure this gets on the next coach out," said Josiah. "And good luck with the trial, sounds like a big one."

Will turned in the doorway as he left, tipping his hat, "Thank you Josiah, it's certainly a big one."

***

As the prosecutor sat down, the tension rested heavily on the courtroom. Over the course of a two-hour opening statement, the prosecutor had described how John Harper, a young lawyer from nearby Independence, Missouri, had shot and killed a man in his own home. He told the jury how Harper, after being arrested for the murder, had escaped jail and fled to New Mexico, only to be returned to Missouri for trial. He painted Harper as a volatile young man. A man who was reckless in his emotions, but cunning enough to meticulously plan a murder.

"You will hear," said the prosecutor, "that Mr. Harper was supposedly acting in self-defense. However, the evidence will show no such thing. Witnesses saw poor young Thomas Meredith walk into the house and within minutes the deadly shot rang out. Hardly time for any provocation of self-defense! In the end," the prosecutor said with fervor, "the evidence will show that Mr. Harper, a man that knows the law and practices in the art of defending murderers, cannot deceive justice or this jury. The state will, therefore, ask that you find Mr. Harper guilty of murder and suffer him the same fate as his unfortunate victim, young Mr. Meredith." The prosecutor turned from the jury, his face a mask of solemnity, and returned to his seat.

It was now Will's turn. He wasn't nervous, as he had given countless opening statements before and had spent many hours preparing for this case. Still, this one seemed different. He was fighting for a man's life as well as the man's family. As he pushed himself up from his chair, rising to his towering height of 6 feet and 5 inches, the desk creaked in the quiet of the courtroom; the remnants of the prosecutor's opening speech still hanging in the air. He walked slowly and deliberately around the table to the jury, looking at each of them in turn. An earnest expression on his face, he began quietly with the words he had practiced so many times. "There are few things in life more precious than life itself. That is true of the life of Mr. Meredith, who died at the end of the tragic quarrel you have already heard about. It is also true of Mr. John Harper, the defendant in this case, who has his whole life ahead of him. And a promising life, indeed, with a loving and devoted wife and family, and the prospect of a great career as an advocate.

"But there is more to the story than what you heard the prosecutor tell you today," said Will as his voice began to rise ever so slightly. "The evidence you will hear is that of a newly arrived aristocrat—a dandy—from the East Coast. Mr. Meredith had his eyes set on going to the frontier to make his fortune, but his eyes got set on something else when he arrived in the Harper home. He had his eyes set on Mr. Harper's wife, the beautiful Fanny

Owens. The Harpers, out of the charity of their hearts, opened their home to this stranger. And how did he repay that charity? By pursuing, relentlessly, the beautiful young Mrs. Harper. In his lascivious pursuit, Mr. Meredith was heedless of the sanctity of marriage or how it would torment Mr. Harper. That's right," Will said sharply to emphasize his point, "this was not a case of inconsequential hard feelings. No, this was the act of a desperate man seeking to protect something possibly more important than life itself—the virtue of a most beloved wife and the bonds of holy matrimony.

"Now he sits before you in this courtroom," Will said gesturing to his client, who looked miserable in his chair, "and he depends on the good judgment of each of you as well as the justice of the law. When the time comes, you will be called upon to decide whether his life is forfeit or whether there are some things that are more important than life itself. I plead with you," Will said with all the earnestness of a close friend, "to judge his heart and set this man free. Free from his anguished actions which were borne of passion for his beloved wife and a noble devotion to her safety and virtue. Free to return to the comfort and society of his family and dear friends."

Finished, Will returned to his seat drained of his emotions but hoping to have laid the foundation for his defense of the case. With years of experience, Will knew how to keep the jury's attention, how to build his defense laying brick after brick of the facts and calling upon the common sense of the jury to consider those facts. Nevertheless, as he sat down, he wondered, as he always did, would it be enough? Would the jury see through the arguments and disagreements, the rash words and hasty actions? As he pondered these questions, he heard the judge strike the gavel and call for adjournment until the following morning, when the prosecution would call its first witness.

***

Returning home that evening, Elizabeth met her husband, Will on the front porch as she often did. "Elizabeth, you're gonna catch a cold out here waiting up for me," said Will.

"Oh, I'm fine," said Elizabeth. "How did the case go today? I've been hearing all about it. My sister Caroline was there in the courtroom and said some of the jurors looked shocked when they learned what that Mr. Meredith fellow was trying to do."

Opening the door, Will conceded, "It did look like my points hit the mark, but it's going to get complicated very soon."

"How so?" asked Elizabeth as she hung up their coats.

"Well, the reason I am late," said Will, "is because we had a long argument with the judge after opening statements. After what I said in opening statements about the man pursuing an affair with Mrs. Harper, the prosecutor made an objection to the judge arguing that we could not put on evidence of criminal intimacy. That is the state's prerogative, the prosecutor argued, to prove a person committed a crime in pursuing another person for illicit relations. We were surprised the judge seriously listened to their argument. Worse still, he agreed with the prosecution. He won't let us ask questions about criminal intimacy."

"What will you do?" asked Elizabeth as they entered the living room together.

"I'm not sure," said Will. "I am afraid we are stuck at the moment. Enough about that," said Will before changing the subject abruptly. "Have we heard anything from Alexander?"

"No," said Elizabeth a little glumly, "but I sent him a letter today."

Will smiled at that, "Actually, I sent him a letter today too."

"Oh, good!" said Elizabeth, "I am sure he will be happy to get any letters. western Virginia is such a long ways away. I hope he is doing well and making friends."

"I'm sure he is," said Will, not quite as confident as his voice suggested. "He makes friends easily, a little too easily I fear sometimes."

"I do wish we had a good college we could send him to that wasn't so far away," said Elizabeth.

"It is interesting that you should say that. I have been in correspondence with some others about bringing a college here to Liberty. It would be a Baptist college, not a Disciples of Christ college, but it would be a great benefit to the area regardless."

"That would be wonderful," exclaimed Elizabeth. "Would it be built in time for Alexander to attend?"

"Oh, I'm not sure," said Will as he unbuttoned his collar, "we are just beginning to talk about it. There is a lot of work yet to do. Dr. William Jewell from Columbia is behind it, though, which is promising." Walking to the kitchen, Will asked, "anything left from dinner?"

"Of course," said Elizabeth. "Let's warm it up a bit."

***

After two days of testimony from the prosecution, it was the defense's turn to put on its case. The plan was to put on four witnesses. The first two witnesses took all morning and described how Mr. Harper had tried to help Mr. Meredith when he arrived from the East Coast. Apparently, Mr. Meredith's plan was to head farther west to California because of the favorable climate and the economic opportunities. But when he arrived in the Harper home, he seemed to lose interest in heading farther west. So he stayed with the Harpers, without working or paying any kind of rent. This bothered the Harpers, but they expected it was just a matter of time before Mr. Meredith headed west.

At the lunch break, Will met with his co-counsel, John Wilson and Silas Woodson, to decide how to proceed. Though they had done well with the witnesses, the critical part of their defense was establishing criminal intimacy. If they were to prove what Will had said in his opening statement, they had to get the evidence in. Under the judge's ruling, though, they could not ask about it.

"Will, I think we just need to ask the judge to reconsider," said Silas, "he's got to come to his senses on this. Without this evidence …" Silas continued.

"I know, I know," said Will, a little frustrated, "our defense is in great danger. I would wager to say that Mr. Harper is going to find himself at the end of a rope if we can't figure this out." Will pinched the bridge of his nose as he thought.

Breaking the silence, John spoke for the first time since sitting down to lunch. "What if we can get the prosecution to raise the issue of criminal intimacy?"

"What was that?" said Will still staring at his boots with his hand on his face.

"Alright, hear me out on this," said John. "The judge only said we could not ask the questions about criminal intimacy. He never said the prosecution couldn't raise the issue. In fact, the prosecutions' whole argument was that it was the state's prerogative to raise criminal intimacy since it is not a defense. It makes perfect sense."

"What makes perfect sense?" asked Silas, not following John's argument.

John, now with more confidence, began again to explain his strategy. "We need to show criminal intimacy, right?"

"Right," said Silas.

"But the judge won't even let us ask about criminal intimacy, right?"

"Right," answered Silas again as if he were being questioned.

"So, we get the prosecution to ask about it!" John said as if he had proven his point.

"And exactly how are we going to get the prosecution to ask about something they objected to already?" Silas asked with finality. The room fell silent at that, and for several minutes defeat settled over them.

Raising his head from his contemplation, Will said quietly, "I think we could do it."

"Do what?" said Silas.

"Exactly what John was just talking about," said Will his eyes now penetrating in their gaze. "We can take them down to the riverbank and put the bait on the hook for them. They're going to want to cast it into the water. They won't be able to resist. Its criminal activity and they are prosecutors. They'll be hooked, and the judge will have to let it in." His mind racing, Will continued, "We're going to need a little time, though, to work out how to get the prosecution to take the bait. I suggest we drag out our final witness today and ask for an adjournment so we can work out how to do it tonight. Can you do that John?"

"I can try," responded John a little unsure. "That is a long time to go with a witness that did not have much to say to begin with."

Fortunately for the defense, the court got started half an hour late following lunch because of another matter before the judge. John then began his questioning slowly, drawing out many details and asking for longer explanations. Several times the prosecution objected, raising concerns as to the point of the lengthy questioning. But just short of irritating the judge and the jury, John finished his examination of the witness at 3:55 p.m. The prosecution, clearly frustrated with the length of the questioning, and seeking to prove a point that the witness' testimony was of no consequence, finished asking questions just after the clock struck 4 o'clock.

At that, Will asked for a conference with the judge and counsel at the bench. "Judge," said Will, "we have one more witness, but the witness is going to take more than the allotted time for today, so I would ask for an adjournment until tomorrow morning. We will finish our witness in the morning and the case can be ready for closing arguments before noon."

Looking to the prosecution, the judge asked, "Any objection?"

"No objection," the prosecutor said as Will breathed a small sigh of relief.

After court was adjourned for the day and the jury shuffled out of the courtroom, Will and his co-counsel gathered in a side room to talk about what to do next. "We have to create some sort of distraction," said Silas now eager to discuss the strategy.

"I agree," said Will, "but what?"

"Well," started John, a sly look on his face, "I know that when I am a little impatient and irritated, I can be distracted. You saw how irritated the prosecution was when we took our time questioning the witness today. I think they are prone to be easily distracted. And if we catch them sleeping …" John continued.

"Wait, what did you say?" Will asked abruptly.

"About getting them distracted?" John asked, a little uncertain.

"No, the sleeping part," said Will. "John, aren't you staying at the same boarding house as the prosecution?"

"Yes," John said, comprehension beginning to dawn.

"Then why don't you spend the evening visiting with the prosecution, talking about the case and seeing how long you can keep them up," suggested Will. "They don't think much is left in the case and they are surely ready for their closing arguments because they think this case is finished, an easy win for them. Let's see how tired they are in the morning, and perhaps we can catch them sleeping."

"Brilliant!" said Silas now filled with energy for the idea.

***

That night Will returned home late again. This time, however, Elizabeth was not on the porch waiting for him. The house was completely dark. Worried he might wake Elizabeth, Will crept quietly into the house and walked into the living room. To his surprise, Elizabeth was lying on the sofa in the darkness, completely dressed, but curled up as if she were asleep.

Just then, a memory flashed in Will's mind. It was a terrible memory from several years ago. He remembered seeing Elizabeth in just this state when she had found out that their oldest son John had died in an accident while visiting a relative. John had a bad toothache and in his excruciating pain in the middle of the night, he had inadvertently taken poison instead of medicine. Though he lingered for a few days, giving hope of a recovery, he ultimately died. The tragedy left Elizabeth debilitated. For weeks, she would not speak to anyone and for months, she had recurrent bouts of melancholia and fits of weeping. Will too, had been devastated. John had so much potential. He was energetic, smart, and was full of life. Then, almost as it were in an instant, he was gone. "How fleeting life can be," Will thought, as a motion in the darkness broke him out of his memories.

It was Elizabeth's hand he had seen in the darkness; she was holding something out to him. It appeared to be a piece of paper. Without a word, he took it from Elizabeth, dread now welling up inside him. Will opened the folded paper. It was a brief letter. With his eyes adjusting to the dark, he made out the words. "Mr. and Mrs. Doniphan, we are sorry to advise you that a terrible accident has happened. Your son, Alexander, in the company of classmates, was swimming across a small stream that was swollen with recent rains. He has gone missing. We have searched for several days unsuccessfully. We are still holding out hope that he will be recovered safe and sound to our care. With our deepest regrets, we send this note. We will alert you of anything we find out as soon as we can. God's blessings. Bethany College."

Will could feel his eyes beginning to sting and a gaping hole expanding in his chest. How could this be? It is not possible! Desperation flooded over him. He wanted to run. But where would he go, what would he do? And what about Elizabeth? Still she had said nothing, she had not even moved. At remembering Elizabeth, his grief subsided to a small degree, and his heart was now filled with anxiety for her.

The death of their oldest son had nearly killed her. Could she bare the loss of their only other child, their precious Alexander? Will knelt and reached out his hand to Elizabeth. Softly their hands touched, and cracking with emotion he whispered, "Elizabeth, oh my sweet Elizabeth, I am so sorry." There was no response and the silence began to expand until it felt like it would engulf the entire world around them. Then, Will felt a gentle pressure on his hand. That small and simple gesture was all Elizabeth could muster, but it was enough. She was there.

The night seemed to simultaneously last forever and to go by in an instant. But the dawn did eventually come. As he woke in the morning, Will's mind raced. He felt helpless with Alexander so far away. They could only wait now for further word. He was determined not to leave Elizabeth alone though. In the morning, he asked Caroline to come stay with Elizabeth, for comfort and companionship. With a heavy heart and trepidation, he headed off to court for what promised to be a turning point in the case.

***

Arriving at the courthouse, his co-counsel John excitedly reported on his evening. "I talked them all the way through the night."

"What?" said Will, forgetting what they had planned the day before.

"You know, the prosecution. We had dinner, played some cards, retold old stories, gossiped," John recited as if it were written on a calendar. "I dare say, the prosecution did not sleep more than a half hour all night."

"Very good," said Will a little more flatly than he intended.

Sensing something had changed, Silas asked, "Will, what's wrong?"

"Nothing, I am well enough," responded Will. "Do you have the questions ready Silas?"

"I do," responded Silas, deciding to let the matter go.

The defense's last witness was a close friend of the Harpers. He described how he witnessed Mr. Meredith become increasingly flirtatious with Mrs. Harper. He saw it at dinners, at gatherings, and he even witnessed it in private moments when Mr. Meredith thought he was alone with Mrs. Harper.

"Did Mr. Meredith show signs of familiarity with the Harpers, especially Mrs. Harper?" asked Silas.

"He did," responded the witness. The witness continued, "I often saw him looking at Mrs. Harper. Now, mind you, Mrs. Harper was not looking back at him and often these were just longing looks from a distance."

At that, Silas expected a fiery objection from the prosecution as he inched closer to the line of questioning about criminal intimacy. None came. Silas peeked over at the prosecution, both of whom had their heads down and appeared not to be paying attention. So he continued, "And on the night of September seventh, did you witness Mrs. Harper in an emotional state running from the barn?"

"I did," said the witness. Then, the witness added unbeckoned, "Moments later I saw Mr. Meredith scurry out of the back of the barn as though he were running from the law." Out of the corner of his eye, Silas saw the lead prosecutor's head snap up and not wanting to press his luck any further, immediately yielded the witness to the prosecution for cross-examination.

Somewhat stunned to be roused out of his stupor by the defense's questions, the prosecutor's instincts kicked in. He asked the first question that came into his mind, "Did you ever personally witness Mr. Meredith imposing himself upon Mrs. Harper in an intimate way?" The witness, so startled by the question, paused for a few moments. And in that instant, the prosecutor realized his mistake. "Don't answer that question!" he shouted, startling both the judge and the jury.

At that, Doniphan rose immediately to his feet, "Your honor, the witness not only should answer the question, but he must answer the question. The prosecutor has asked the question of criminal intimacy in the hearing of the jury, and they are entitled to hear the answer."

"Counsel, please approach the bench," said the judge.
The judge excused the jury so that the argument was not in their presence. For nearly an hour, counsel argued about the matter before the judge. In the end, the judge determined the prosecution had opened the door in front of the jury by asking a question about criminal intimacy. Therefore, the witness was permitted to answer the question.

When the jury returned, the question was repeated and the witness said, "What I witnessed was a woman hurriedly leaving a barn. She was clearly distraught, her hair and clothes disheveled."

"Did you see who that woman was?" the prosecutor asked.

"Yes!" the witness said with conviction, "it was Mrs. Harper."

"But that was all you saw, right?" asked the prosecutor, hoping to end the story at that.

"No," the witness continued, "moments after I saw Mrs. Harper leave the barn, a man skulked out of the back of the barn. It was Mr. Meredith, I am certain."

The prosecutor, now flustered by the witnesses' answers, tried to get the questioning back on track, saying, "But again, you did not see what had happened."

"Well, I did not see Mr. Meredith impose himself upon this married woman, if that is your question, but that is what it looked like." Then, the witness added, gratuitously, "If that were my wife, I would have gone after that scoundrel." At that, the prosecutor objected and moved to strike the response. The judge sustained the motion, but the damage was done.

In closing arguments, the prosecution focused on the facts of the case. The timing of the shooting, the witnesses who saw Mr. Meredith go into the house, the shots heard moments later, and Mr. Meredith being found dead. The prosecution's delivery was straightforward but hollow, almost defeated. Finally, the prosecutor asked the jury, "If you value the law, civility, and justice, then you must convict Mr. Harper of murder. People, even lawyers, cannot take justice into their own hands as they see fit. It matters not that Mr. Meredith was newly arrived from the East Coast, or that he was a guest in the Harper's home. What matters is the law." After delivering his speech, the prosecutor fell into his chair and yielded the floor to the defense.

Will started his oration from his chair. "Esteemed jurors; let us agree that Mr. Meredith was shot and that he was shot after a short argument with Mr. Harper. That is not the question. The question is—why? And when you consider that question, I want you to imagine Mr. Harper's terrible position. He welcomed Mr. Meredith with open arms. He opened his home to this person, trusting that he was a law-abiding gentleman. Mr. Meredith was well educated and appeared to be possessed of good manners. Everything Mr. Harper had, in a material sense, he willingly offered to this man. What he did not offer, and what he never expected, however, was that Mr. Meredith would take his generosity to the point of criminal intimacy with his beloved wife."

Not wanting to lose the passions of the jury with repetition or overemphasis, Will summarized the salient facts in less than half an hour, and concluded with these words: "Mr. Harper, learning of the sophistry and indecency of Mr. Meredith was a tormented man. Imagine what he must have felt, and ask yourself this question, what is more important than life itself? If you can answer, the care and safety of a beloved wife, daughter or … son," Will said, his voice catching with emotion on the mention of a son. Collecting himself, Will concluded with his plea, "If that be the case, then you must find that Mr. Harper is not guilty and should be permitted to live out his life in the company of his family and in the marital felicity that is his God-given right. Thank you."

As Will returned to his seat, he could see emotion in the faces of the jury and from the gallery there were intermittent sniffs and tears in the eyes of some. The jury was then left to deliberate on the matter and return their verdict. As soon as the jury left the chambers, Will grabbed his hat and coat and headed for the door.

Silas, reaching to shake his hand and congratulate him on a masterful closing argument, asked, "Where are you going Will? With that kind of closing argument, the jury could come back soon."

"I've got to go home."

"Why, what's wrong?" Silas asked as he did earlier in the morning, real concern now in his voice.

"I'm sorry but it's my son Alexander, he's missing," Will said as he hastily turned to leave. Both Silas and John, looked at each other in surprise, as their friend Will made his way through the crowd shaking hands with well-wishers wanting to meet the great lawyer and war hero.

***

For the next hour, the lawyers chatted with each other and the judge as they waited for word from the jury. At home, Will was greeted by his wife Elizabeth, who was surrounded by family and friends. "No news," she said even before Will could ask. The big case, the case that had so consumed their conversations over the past few weeks, was never mentioned, even at this critical moment. Instead, their conversation was about their son and when word would come from western Virginia. After what seemed like mere moments, a messenger came from the courthouse to report that the jury had reached their verdict and would soon return to the courtroom to deliver it. Will, embraced his wife and made his way back to the courthouse.

With the parties and lawyers back in the courtroom, the judge summoned the jury. "All rise," the judge said as the jury filed into the jury box. "You may be seated."

"Have you reached a verdict?" the judge asked the jury, not directing the question to any particular juror.

"Yes," came a voice from the second row, a large man who was a local farmer.

"Are you the jury foreman?" asked the judge.

"Yes," said the same juror reaching out his hand with a piece of paper.

The judge directed the courtroom bailiff to retrieve the verdict. The judge quickly read the verdict to himself as everyone in the courtroom waited in silence. Then, looking up at the jury foreman asked, "Is this the verdict of the jury?"

"Yes," said the jury foreman again, adding, "it is unanimous."

"Very well," said the judge. He then turned to the lawyers and the defendant. "Please rise. On the charge of murder," the judge read, "we the jury find the defendant, John Harper, not guilty."

Mr. Harper, who had remained impassive throughout most of the trial, broke down when he heard the words. His wife, sitting in the row behind him came to him and they embraced as all around the courtroom people broke into excited conversations and even a smattering of applause. At that, the judge struck his gavel, calling the court to order. "Quiet in the courtroom," he said, "we are not quite finished." He continued, "In accordance with the jury's verdict, judgment is hereby entered in favor of the defendant. I thank the jury for their service and the lawyers and witnesses for a well-tried case. Court is now adjourned."

For the next half hour, Will accepted the congratulations of lawyers and onlookers alike. All the while, his mind remained at home with his family and his wife Elizabeth. He recited "thank you, that's very kind of you," dozens of times. Yet, he could feel the exhaustion of the trial and the strain of worry about his son settling over him. Finally, mercifully, Silas interceded, so that Will could collect his things and leave the courtroom. As he did, he could not help but wonder how the trial of his own life would turn out. Would he be permitted to enjoy the fellowship of his wife and son or was he to struggle as so many others had in losing loved ones on the frontier?

***

Over the next two weeks, the Doniphans waited with anxiety to hear further word of their son. Then, the news they feared finally came. Alexander's body had been found down river. Having braced for this most heartbreaking news, the Doniphans had already begun to cope. Unfortunately, Elizabeth could not bear the grief. She ultimately suffered a debilitating stroke. Will would faithfully care for her the rest of her life, knowing the terrible burden she bore.

His beloved Elizabeth died on July 19, 1873 and was laid to rest in Liberty, Missouri. In the years that followed, Will reflected repeatedly upon the course of his life and the things that matter most. He had saved many lives and families in his time, but the question kept coming back to him, "Are there things that really do matter more than life itself?" As he bore the burden of watching the lives of those he loved cut short, he concluded it must be true.

Life is fleeting, but love and family are not. They are forever.

The Influence of Alexander William Doniphan

CHAPTER 11

Alexander W. Doniphan on National Television: The NBC Nationwide Telecast of Profiles in Courage

Alexander L. Baugh, Brigham Young University

After the election of John F. Kennedy as President of the United States, television executive Robert Saudek developed a television series based on and inspired by Kennedy's Pulitzer Prize winning book, Profiles in Courage. Episode 10 of the series was about Alexander Doniphan and his role in the Mormon War in Missouri. The episode aired nationwide on January 17, 1965. For many in the United States, this was likely the first time they learned about Doniphan.

Chapter Page Image: A highly stylized lithograph depicting the court martial of the leaders of the Latter-day Saints. -- Carter, C. W. (circa 1885). *The Extermination of the Latter Day Saints from the State of Missouri in the Fall of 1838 [Photograph]*. Church History Catalog, Church of Jesus Christ of Latter-day Saints, Salt Lake City, UT.

In 1956, thirty-nine year-old John F. Kennedy, the junior Senator from Massachusetts, published *Profiles in Courage: Decisive Moments in the Lives of Celebrated Americans*, a 287-page book highlighting episodes in the lives of eight U.S. Senators who exhibited uncharacteristic political valor and who defied the opinions of their political party and constituents to do what they felt was right, only to suffer criticism and losses in popularity because of their actions. The book featured such notables as John Quincy Adams (Massachusetts), Daniel Webster (Massachusetts), Thomas Hart Benton (Missouri's own "Old Bullion"), and Sam Houston (Texas), but a few lesser knowns—Edmund G. Ross (Kansas), Lucius Quintus Cincinnatus Lamar (Mississippi), George W. Norris (Nebraska), and Robert A. Taft (Ohio).[1] Kennedy was assisted by a number of scholars, editors, and librarians who facilitated his research and writing.[2] The book became a bestseller, and in 1957, he received the Pulitzer Prize for biography. After his Presidential election in 1960, an "Inaugural" edition of the book appeared in 1961, and following his assassination in 1964, a "Memorial" edition was published.

Profiles in Courage – The Television Series

Capitalizing on the popularity of Kennedy's book, as well as his presidency, Robert Saudek, an innovative network executive and an experienced creator of a number of award-winning cultural radio and television programs, came up with the idea to produce a television series adaptation of the book by the same name, Profiles in Courage, consisting of twenty-six episodes. He ran the idea by Kennedy, who gave his approval, and in June 1963, Saudek struck a deal with NBC to air the series on national television. He also headed up the production team as executive producer of the series.[3]

Since each episode would be based on a specific historical American figure, Saudek needed the help of a professional historian who could serve as a consultant for the series. That person was Allan Nevins, a distinguished emeritus professor of history at Columbia University and a two-time recipient of the Pulitzer Prize for history.[4] Nevins had also written the foreword to the 1961 edition of Kennedy's book.

Saudek looked primarily to Nevins to recommend individuals in American history who exemplified uncommon courage and heroism to be featured in the twenty-six episodes. Saudek and his production team eventually settled on highlighting seven of the eight men in Kennedy's book (Lucius Quintus Cincinnatus Lamar was not chosen) along with nineteen others. Of the remaining nineteen, six were prominent American statesmen—George Mason, John Adams, John Marshall, Frederick Douglass, Andrew Johnson, and Grover Cleveland. But the remaining thirteen were considerably less prominent, and for the most part would have been relatively unknown by most Americans—John Peter Altgeld, Thomas Corwin, Prudence Crandall, Richard T. Ely, Hamilton Fish, Anne Hutchison, Charles Evan Hughes, Benjamin Barr Lindsey, Mary S. McDowell, John M. Slayton, Oscar Underwood, and last but not least, Alexander W. Doniphan, who had gained prominence in Missouri in the mid-nineteenth century, but was less widely known in later times. With half of the individuals featured in the television series being relatively obscure historical figures, it seems that Nevins played a prominent role in the individuals who were ultimately selected.[5] He also reviewed each of the screenplay scripts for historical accuracy, once again suggesting that he had a heavy hand in their selection. Significantly, all the historical figures chosen for the series were approved by Kennedy before his assassination.

By 1963, Nevins had enjoyed an illustrious fifty year career in journalism and history, having distinguished himself as one of the foremost scholars of American history in the country, having published over a thousand articles, authored some fifty books, and edited another seventy-five volumes.[6] In his study of U.S. history, he had become well acquainted with Missouri history, particularly during the antebellum period. Part of his familiarity with Missouri stemmed from researching and writing a two-volume biography on John Charles Fremont, a son-in-law of Missouri's powerful Senator Thomas Hart Benton (who was also included in Kennedy's book and in the TV series). No doubt in his study of Missouri's early decades, Nevins learned of Alexander Doniphan's notoriety and achievements as a successful defense attorney, three-term representative in the state legislature, brigadier general in the regional and state militia, commanding officer of the First Missouri Mounted Volunteer Regiment in the Mexican War, his role as a leading figure in the state's Whig party, and as a political adversary and critic of Missouri Senator Thomas Benton.[7] In addition, in his Missouri studies, Nevins would have also become familiar with Doniphan's role as chief legal counsel to the Latter-day Saints living in Missouri in the 1830s, and his courageous defense of the Mormons and their leaders during what became known as the 1838 Missouri Mormon War. It was at that time in Doniphan's career that he was caught in the middle. During the civil conflict between the Mormons and their non-Mormon neighbors, he served as a brigadier general in the regional and state militia that was called out to maintain civil order, while simultaneously serving as the chief legal counsel to the Mormons and their leaders. This dichotomy provided Nevins and the producers of the television series with the ideal historical setting (the Mormon War) and the historical figure (Doniphan) to feature in a *Profiles in Courage* episode.

The Screenplay

Writer Don M. Mankiewicz received the contract to produce the screenplay for the Doniphan episode.[8] At the time, no descriptive full-length biography had been written about Doniphan; most likely, Mankiewicz was probably not even familiar with who he was. He would likely have known something about the Mormons, but probably little, if anything, about their history during the 1830s when they established several settlements in Missouri, and the controversy surrounding the 1838 conflict. Where he obtained the historical information to write the screenplay could not be accurately determined. He may have read about Doniphan and the 1838 Mormon conflict from general histories published about the state. He likely used material from the *History of Caldwell and Daviess Counties* (1886). Historian Allan Nevins may have also provided Mankiewicz with some biographical information about Doniphan as well as historical sources about the Mormons.[9]

A major challenge of any screenwriter is to tell a story in a limited amount of time. Each *Profile of Courage episode* was geared to fit in a sixty-minute time slot, while also allowing for commercials. The screenplay Mankiewicz drafted would have been reviewed, edited, and then approved by Nevins, as well as the producer, director, and production staff for content and clarity before actual production could begin. The final cut of the show ended up being close to fifty minutes in length (49:40 to be exact, which allowed approximately ten minutes for commercials), consisting of twenty-five separate scenes (including the introduction, film credits and the ending).

Production

Paul Stanley directed the episode. Patricia Rose was the casting director.[10] Together, the two likely had the major say in the cast selection. Significantly, Peter Lawford, a popular Hollywood actor, who had played leading roles in numerous film and television productions, was cast in the leading role of Alexander W. Doniphan. (Ironically, Lawford was also a brother-in-law to President John F. Kennedy, having married Patricia Kennedy, a younger sister to the president.) Each of the other main cast members were also veteran television and movie actors.

Actor	*Character*
Peter Lawford	Alexander W. Doniphan, Clay County lawyer, chief legal counsel for the Mormons, and brigadier general in regional and state militia
Michael Constantine	Samuel D. Lucas, major general in the regional and state militia from Jackson County
Simon Oakland	Samuel Bogart, captain in the Ray County militia
Robert Emhardt	Missouri Governor Lilburn W. Boggs

James Callahan	Major Barnes aide to Alexander W. Doniphan (fictitious)
George Lindsey	Adam Black, justice of the peace in Daviess County
Paul Stevens	Joseph Smith, Prophet and President of The Church of Jesus Christ of Latter-day Saints
Tim O'Connor	Sidney Rigdon, First Counselor in the First Presidency of The Church of Jesus Christ of Latter-day Saints
Don Collier	George M. Hinkle, Mormon colonel in the regional militia and commander of the Mormon forces in Caldwell County

All of these actors went on to have other major roles in both motion pictures and television.

All twenty-six episodes of *Profiles in Courage* were filmed in black and white at Desilu Studios in Culver City, California. While all the indoor scenes for the Doniphan episode would have been filmed in one of the studio's soundstages, a number of scenes were shot outdoors, presumably in a rural area in the vicinity of Los Angeles. Production of the entire episode probably took several weeks or months. "General Alexander W. Doniphan" aired on primetime television (NBC-TV) nationwide on Sunday evening January 17, 1965, at 6:30 p.m. (Eastern Time), immediately after *Meet the Press,* and before *Disney's Wonderful World of Color.*[11] The episode was the tenth in the *Profiles in Courage* series.[12]

Scene Descriptions

The opening scene begins with Sidney Rigdon, a counselor to Joseph Smith, Jr. speaking at the July 4, 1838 celebration by the Mormons at the town of Far West, Caldwell County, Missouri. In his patriotic, yet fiery remarks, Rigdon breaks out into a denunciation against the individuals and groups in Missouri who, for many years, had persecuted the Mormons. For them, Rigdon declares, "It shall be a war of extermination!" Those assembled respond with angry cries and shouts of approval, whereupon Doniphan intervenes, and requests Joseph Smith, Jr. put an end to the group's raucous behavior (Scene 1). In terms of the actual history, Doniphan was not present on the occasion, nonetheless, Mankiewicz wrote him into the script to illustrate Doniphan's role throughout the rest of the episode as one who sought to secure and maintain peace between the Mormons, their antagonistic Missouri neighbors, and the civil and military authorities.

Following the introduction and credits to the *Profiles in Courage* series (Scenes 2 and 3), the next scene shows Missouri Governor Lilburn W. Boggs in his office in Jefferson City, Missouri, discussing the Mormon problem with Samuel D. Lucas, a major general in the state militia from Jackson County, and Samuel Bogart, a captain in the Ray County militia (Scene 4). Historically, this meeting never took place, but Mankiewicz probably wrote the scene into the screenplay to illustrate the growing concern over the outbreaks and disturbances between the Mormons and their northern Missouri neighbors.

Scene 5 centers around a fight that broke out on August 6, 1838, at the election polls in Gallatin, the county seat of Daviess County, between a group of local citizens and a small band of Mormons who lived nearby in the Mormon settlement of Adam-ondi-Ahman. Mankiewicz places Doniphan at the polls (although historically he was not there), and when the fight breaks out, once again Doniphan intercedes and quells the disturbance (Scene 5). Two days after the fracas, Mormon leaders visit Adam Black, a Daviess County justice of the peace, demanding that he agree to protect the rights of the Mormons (Scene 6). Black responded by issuing a complaint against Joseph Smith and several other Mormon leaders. A preliminary hearing is held against Smith and several other Mormon defendants who are represented in the court proceedings by Doniphan as their defense attorney (Scene 7). The depiction of these three scenes are fairly historically accurate, the most notable exceptions being that Doniphan was not present at the Gallatin skirmish, and while he is also portrayed as the attorney who represented the Mormon leaders at the hearing (and he was present), the defendants were actually represented on that occasion by David Rice Atchison, Doniphan's law partner.

At this point, Mankiewicz's screenplay skips over several major incidents in the Missouri-Mormon conflict that took place in late August, September, and most of October, and jumps to the events associated with the Battle of Crooked River that took place on the evening and early morning hours October 24–25, 1838, in northern Ray County (Scenes 8–13). Samuel Bogart, captain of the Ray County militia, receives authorization to patrol the county line separating Ray and Caldwell counties (Scene 8), followed by three fictitious scenes that set the stage for the encounter (Scenes 9–11). While on patrol, Bogart's men come across a company of Mormons from Caldwell County, and a clash takes place, resulting in the deaths of one Missourian and three Mormon defenders

(Scene 12). An exaggerated report of the incident is dispatched to Governor Boggs who responds by issuing an executive order in the presence of Lucas stating that "the Mormons must be treated as enemies and must be exterminated or driven from the state if necessary for the public good." He also authorizes Lucas to call out several regiments of the state militia to execute the Extermination Order against the Mormons (Scene 13).

The stage is now set for the showdown between Doniphan and major general Samuel D. Lucas. Lucas is camped with a state militia force south of Far West with the intention of carrying out the governor's orders. Doniphan, who by this time has been activated into militia service with the rank of brigadier general (the rank just below that of Lucas), meets with Lucas and the two officers argue over what the governor meant by the order. The question is whether the governor meant that the Mormons were to actually be "exterminated," or did he mean they were to be driven from the state? Lucas thought the former, Doniphan the latter. But Doniphan also considered the entire order to be illegal, thereby leading to a standstill between the two men (Scene 14). Meanwhile, with the presence of a large force of state militia camped near Far West, Mormon leaders consider their options (Scene 15). At this point, Doniphan convinces Lucas to negotiate a surrender with Mormon leaders rather than engage in armed conflict (Scene 16). Bogart is sent to meet with Hinckle, commander of the Mormon forces, and informs him of the terms of the surrender (Scene 17). Hinckle returns to Far West and tells Joseph Smith Jr. and Sidney Rigdon that Lucas wants to meet to consider the terms of surrender and Smith agrees to go (Scene 18). However, when Smith and the other Mormon leaders arrive at General Lucas's field headquarters, Lucas immediately places the Mormon leaders under arrest and orders a court martial hearing (Scene 19). In the hearing, Joseph Smith Jr. and several other Mormon leaders are found guilty of treason. Lucas then issues the following order to Doniphan: "General Doniphan, you will take Joseph Smith and the others to the public square at Far West and shoot them at nine o'clock this morning. By my order, S.D. Lucas—general, commanding."[13] Lucas hands Doniphan the copy of the order, which he refuses to take. Lucas reacts by calmly telling him, "You have just two hours, general." Doniphan remains motionless, causing Lucas to become visibly angry before shouting at the top of his voice: "Is the order understood?" Unruffled, Doniphan calmly replies, "Understood" (Scene 20).

The next scene shows Doniphan considering his options—either observe the order and execute the Mormon leaders, or refuse the order and risk being charged with insubordination, followed by a court martial and possible execution (Scene 21). In a dramatic scene, the episode reaches its climax. Doniphan approaches Lucas and boldly confronts him. "General, what you propose is cold-blooded murder. I will not obey your order. My brigade is leaving for Liberty now. If you execute those men, I will hold you responsible before an earthly tribunal, so help me God!"[14] There is dead silence. Lucas is speechless, and Doniphan bravely walks away (Scene 22).

Doniphan is next silhouetted against the Missouri skyline as the narrator pays the following tribute:

> Alexander William Doniphan's political life was curtailed by his association with the unpopular Mormon cause. But he had a long career at the bar, and he did indeed contribute to the growth of the country. In 1847,

during the Mexican War, Doniphan led his brigade on a spectacularly successful campaign. But his courage had been proven for all time in a less glamorous, bloodless battle against intangible enemies, himself included, at dawn on a Missouri hillside (Scene 23).

The closing scene concludes with a short narration on the essence and embodiment of human courage recorded by President John F. Kennedy before his death: "These stories of past courage can teach, they can offer hope, and they can provide personal inspiration. But they cannot supply courage itself. For this, each man must look into his own soul" (Scene 24). The movie ends with the film's credits being shown accompanied by a band playing a spirited Irish martial ballad (Scene 25).

Assessment

The Doniphan episode, like all the episodes in the Profiles in Courage television series, was essentially a historical docudrama—a dramatized television movie based on real individuals and actual events in history. Given that the episode was intended to be a dramatization or adaptation, the screenwriter, Mankiewicz, could have some literary license with the screenplay. For example, in creating the script he depicted scenes and created events that did not actually happen. He also took the liberty to produce conversational dialogue, simply because in most instances he could not have known what the original characters literally spoke or said. The same leeway applied to the director regarding how the various scenes were interpreted and depicted, as well as to the actors in how the characters they played were portrayed. Mankiewicz's main goal was to reconstruct a relevant historical storyline, place the characters into the setting, and construct a narrative and dialogue, whereupon, the director, together with the actors, would work to capture as much as possible the authentic nature and qualities of the individuals being portrayed.

The most glaring historical misrepresentation in the episode was Mankiewicz's inclusion of Samuel D. Lucas as the main nemesis against the Mormons. And although he detested the Latter-day Saints and their leaders (Lucas was from Jackson County, where the Mormons had lived from 1831 to 1833), he did not play a role in the 1838 conflict until after October 27, when Governor Boggs issued the Extermination Order and called out the regional and state militia to subdue the Mormons. In an executive order issued by the governor on October 26, just the day before, Boggs relieved Major General David Rice Atchison (who was sympathetic to the Mormons), the regional commander of the 3rd Division of the state militia from his duties. And it was Atchison, not Lucas, who had been in charge of the regional forces during the civil disturbances up until this time (August through late October). In the October 26 order, Boggs replaced Atchison with John B. Clark of Howard County, however it would be over a week before Clark would arrive at Far West. In the meantime, with Atchison gone, Lucas, who held the same rank as Atchison (major general) and the highest ranking officer in the field at the time, assumed command of the regional forces until Clark would arrive.[15] During the entire first half of the episode, Mankiewicz mistakenly or incorrectly makes it appear as if Lucas was the leading antagonist against the Mormons and that it was he who conspired to remove them from the state, when in fact, Lucas did not play a role in the conflict until it was almost over. Mankiewicz's screenplay could have been much more historically accurate had he included depictions of David Rice Atchison's role in the conflict. However, to his credit, Mankiewicz's screenplay of Lucas' demands regarding the surrender terms, his meeting with Joseph Smith Jr. and other Mormon leaders, the subsequent court martial, and his order to Doniphan to shoot the prisoners was powerful and moving.

Individuals who have studied Doniphan's life, and who are also familiar with his association with the Latter-day Saints and his involvement in the 1838 Mormon conflict, could easily find dozens of other inaccurate historical details in the episode. However, despite the film's deficiencies, Mankiewicz's screenplay, along with Paul Stanley's artistic directing, and most of all, Lawford's superb portrayal of Doniphan, altogether captured to a remarkable degree, the persona, essence, integrity, and impeccable character of Alexander W. Doniphan. In addition, the episode also helped the viewing audience understand to some extent, the political, social, and religious intolerance that characterized this period of American history.

Northern Missouri counties, communities, and settlements at the time of the 1838 Missouri-Mormon conflict. -- *Map Courtesy John Hamer*

Leading actors in the "General Alexander W. Doniphan" episode of Profiles in Courage. -- Photo Courtesy The Film Collectors Society of America. https://www.thefilmcsa.com/

Endnotes

1. John F. Kennedy, *Profiles in Courage: Decisive Moments in the Lives of Celebrated Americans,* 1st edition (New York: Harper, 1956).

2. Although Kennedy is celebrated as the author of the book, Theodore (Ted) C. Sorenson, a Kennedy speech writer, wrote most of the book. See Daniel Marcus, "Profiles in Courage: Television History on the New Frontier," in *Television Histories: Shaping Collective Memory in the Media Age,* ed. Gary R. Edgerton and Peter C. Rollins (Lexington: University of Kentucky Press, 2001), 81.

3. Marcus, "Profiles in Courage," 85. In the 1940s and 50s, Robert Saudek was an executive vice-president of ABC. For information on Saudek's television credits see Robert Thomas Jr., "Robert Saudek Is Dead at 85; A Pioneer of Culture on TV," *New York Times,* March 17, 1997, Section B, p. 9. See also "Robert Saudek" at https://en.wikipedia.org/wiki/Robert_Saudek_(television_executive)

4. Marcus, "Profiles in Courage," 86. Nevins's name appears in the credit lines at the end of each episode as the historical consultant.

5. Two of the historical figures chosen to be featured in the television series were Grover Cleveland and Hamilton Fish. Nevins wrote full-length biographies on both of these individuals (he won the Pulitzer Prize in history for both), supporting the idea that he played a role in the selection of the characters who would be featured in the television series.

6. See Ray Allen Billington, *Allan Nevins on History* (New York: Scribner's, 1975).

7. Alexander W. Doniphan's life and his achievements are chronicled in the full-length biography by Roger G. Launius, *Alexander William Doniphan: Portrait of a Missouri Moderate* (Columbia, University of Missouri Press, 1997).

8. Don M. Mankiewicz (1922–2015) was a popular screenwriter for both television and the motion picture industries. His many television credits include writing episodes for *Star Trek, Mannix, Ironside,* and *Marcus Welby, M.D.* See https://en.wikipedia.org/wiki/Don_Mankiewicz. Mankiewicz's name appears as the writer in the credits at the beginning of the "General Alexander W. Doniphan" episode. In addition to writing the screenplay for "General Alexander W. Doniphan," Mankiewicz, was the screenwriter for five other episodes in the *Profiles in Courage* television series, the most of any of the screenwriters. See https://www.imdb.com/title/tt0057780/fullcredits?ref_=tt_cl_sm#cast.

9. While it is not precisely known what historical sources Mankiewicz examined to write the screenplay, it is significant to note that many of the scenes, events, main characters, and locations depicted in the episode follow the general historical narrative found in *History of Caldwell and Livingston Counties, Missouri* (St. Louis:

National Historical Company, 1886), chapter 3, "The Mormon War, pages 124–144, which suggests Mankiewicz likely referred to the information in the chapter.

10. Paul Stanley is listed in the opening credits of the film, Rose in the credits at the end. For over three decades, Stanley directed several motion pictures and episodes for notable television series such as *Gunsmoke, MacGyver, Charlie's Angels, Dallas, The Love Boat, The Six Million Dollar Man, Hawaii Five-0*, and *Mission: Impossible* to name a few. See https://www.imdb.com/name/nm0822570/

11. Marcus, "Profiles in Courage," 85.

12. The first episode of *Profiles in Courage,* featuring Oscar W. Underwood, a U.S. Senator who opposed the Klu Klux Klan, premiered November 8, 1964. The last episode, the twenty-sixth, aired on May 9, 1965. The episodes were broadcast on NBC every successive Sunday during this period with the exception of November 22, 1964, making the total run was twenty-seven weeks. See https://en.wikipedia.org/wiki/Profiles_in_Courage_(TV_series). A digitally mastered copy of the entire episode was acquired by purchase online. See https://www.thefilmcsa.com/princoratvse.html

13. The lines used by Lucas (Constantine) ordering Doniphan (Lawford) to execute the Mormon leaders closely aligns with the actual order Lucas gave to Doniphan following the court martial hearing: "Brigadier-General Doniphan.—Sir: You will take Joseph Smith and the other prisoners into the public square at Far West, and shoot them at 9 o'clock to-morrow morning. Samuel D. Lucas, Major-General Commanding." The copy of the original manuscript of the order has not been located. However, the text for the order was first published in *History of Caldwell and Livingston Counties, Missouri,* 137, published in 1886 a year before Doniphan's death (1887), suggesting that the compilers of the volume had access to the original document.

14. The lines used by Doniphan (Lawford) refusing to comply with the execution order of Lucas (Constantine) also match up closely with the actual reply Doniphan issued in his refusal to execute the prisoners: "It is cold-blooded murder. I will not obey your order. My brigade shall march for liberty to-morrow morning, at 8 o'clock; and if you execute those men, I will hold you responsible before an earthly tribunal, so help me God! A.W. Doniphan, Brigadier-General." See *History of Caldwell and Livingston Counties, Missouri,* 137, and previous note.

15. For a definitive study and analysis of the 1838 Missouri-Mormon conflict, see Alexander L. Baugh, *A Call to Arms: The 1838 Mormon Defense of Northern Missouri* (Provo, UT: Joseph Fielding Smith Institute for Latter-day Saint History and BYU Studies, 2000).

ALEXANDER L. BAUGH is a professor and current chair of the Department of Church History and Doctrine at Brigham Young University. He received his BS from Utah State University, and his MA and PhD degrees from BYU. He specializes in researching and writing about the Missouri period of early LDS Church history (1831–1839). He is a member of the Mormon History Association and the John Whitmer Historical Association, having served as president of that organization in 2006–2007. He is also the past editor of Mormon Historical Studies, and past co-director of research for the BYU Religious Studies Center.

CHAPTER 12

Influential Missourian Alexander Doniphan

Steven V. Potter

A short essay on the influence of Alexander Doniphan.

Chapter Page Image: Alexander Doniphan statue at the Ray County Courthouse taken in 1918. -- Hibbard, F. C. (1918). Alexander W. Doniphan Monument [B/w photo]. Retrieved July, 2020, from State Historical Society of Missouri https://digital.shsmo.org/digital/collection/imc/id/22743/rec/2

Who is the most well-known Missourian? Sheryl Crow or Brad Pitt? How about the most influential Missourian? Harry Truman or Chuck Berry? For many years, I have believed that the least recognized but most influential Missourian is Alexander Doniphan.

It is true that the Doniphan name has resurfaced in Clay County, Missouri, and people recognize the highway and school that bear his name? However, why is he important to people today? Regardless of his personal opinion, Doniphan always seemed to do what was needed even if it was not popular. Doniphan embodied these qualities, which I believe were unique in the nineteenth century but equally unique today.

In the 1830s, Doniphan, who was also a general in the Missouri militia, was ordered in the field to carry out an order to exterminate the leaders of the Mormon Church in Missouri. Although under orders, Doniphan refused to execute these men. Doniphan, who was not a Mormon, defended these men in court and secured their safe passage out of the state. For Doniphan, it wasn't about fearing someone different from you, but about doing what was right.

When America went to war against Mexico in 1846, Doniphan responded to the call. He commanded a military campaign of over 5,000 miles and helped secure the trade routes to Santa Fe, New Mexico. To this day, much of the New Mexico code of laws is based on the code Doniphan wrote for the area following the war. Under direction from General Stephen W. Kearny, Doniphan wrote a code in English and Spanish for all the people of the new territory. For Doniphan, it was about creating a set of rules that everyone could understand—not just the winners.

Doniphan believed in education. In 1849, the Missouri Baptist Convention decided to establish a college in Boonville, Missouri. Doniphan, who was not Baptist, joined with several prominent Baptists in Clay County to persuade the founding of William Jewell College in Liberty, Missouri. Doniphan also served as the first superintendent of the Liberty Public Schools. For Doniphan, it was about supporting education—not just supporting people who thought as he did.

We need more people like Alexander Doniphan. We need people that can abandon their "tribe" and do what is right for the community...even if it is unpopular.

Originally published on Wednesday, 08/15/2018 - 10:31am on Mid-Continent Public Library, From the Director Blog (mymcpl.org/blogs/director-influential-missourian-alexander-doniphan)

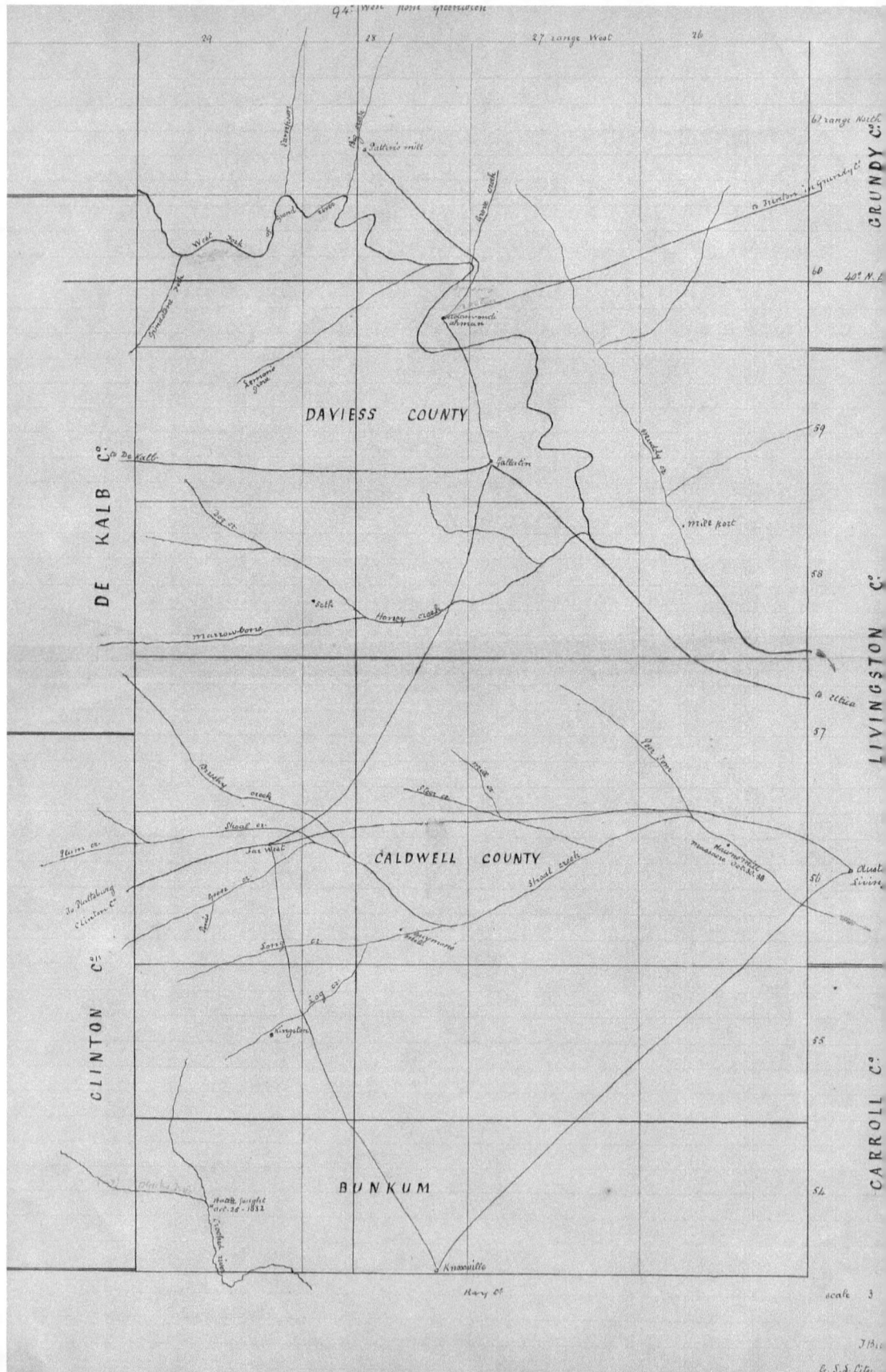

CHAPTER 13

The History of Caldwell County

Caldwell County Missouri Website[1]

From the Caldwell County, Missouri website, this article explains the early history of Caldwell County, and the role Alexander W. Doniphan had in helping create this unique place. (Permission for this article was granted by Presiding Commissioner, Bud Motsinger, April 20, 2020)

Chapter Page Image: Map of Caldwell and Davies Counties drawn in 1862. -- Bullock, T. (1862). Thomas Bullock Maps of Missouri [Representations of the counties of Jackson, Clay, Caldwell and Daviess, with notations as to early Mormon settlements and history. Drawn by Thomas Bullock at the request of Church historian George A. Smith. Verso of both maps contain draft copies of Utah Territory legislative acts for 1862.]. Retrieved July, 2020, from Church History Catalog, Church of Jesus Christ of Latter-day Saints https://catalog.churchofjesuschrist.org/assets?id=1333e1ec-a8eb-4528-aa31-41e0d635a41d&crate=0&index=0

The history of Caldwell County actually begins on a sad note with a large group of people looking for a place to escape religious persecution and ultimately somewhere they could call home. The Mormon Saints under the direction of their "prophet" leader Joseph Smith Jr. had been exiled from Independence, Missouri.

They had fled to Clay County for safety and were at first treated with kindness and respect. However, Clay County citizens offered their county only as a temporary refuge for the Latter-Day Saints. They were anxious for them to move on! When vigilantes began gathering in large numbers and a county war seemed imminent, Clay's leading citizens met with Mormon leaders and asked them to leave the county.

One of the influential residents in Liberty was one Alexander W. Doniphan, a representative elect of Clay County. He saw a need to protect the innocent women and children, so he prepared and introduced into the legislature a bill to organize a county designated specifically for the Mormon Saints. (It was named after Captain Matthew Caldwell, who was General Doniphan's father's respected commander in the Revolution.)[2]

Some of the settlers in the area argued that Mormon settlements would "hinder[3] the prosperity of the county, check future emigration of any other class except the Mormons and disturb the peace of our community." As a result of this opposition, the proposed boundaries for Caldwell County were reduced by more than half forming a second county to the north called Daviess. Most of the non-Mormon settlers in Caldwell, about twenty in number, sold their farms and moved out.

The Northern part of Ray County was sparsely inhabited. It was an ideal place for the Saints to live in freedom. Even though it was mostly rolling prairie, there were lush grasses, plenty of water and excellent hunting. The land was ideal for the industrious pioneers. They had already been hardened by trials. Their faith in God, and their zeal for the new gospel they had found would strengthen them for the work ahead. The land could be purchased for a small amount of money. Most considered it wasteland. Awaiting the approval by the legislature, some Saints moved to the sparsely populated area in Ray County along the Crooked River. A sizeable settlement of Mormons developed in the Rock Ford area.

Some came ahead and began the work of preparing a place for the new inhabitants. One of them was Jacob Haun, who was bringing his family. He began construction on the famed "Haun's Mill." (The mill was built in 1834.)

On December 26, 1836, CALDWELL COUNTY WAS BORN! A location between Goose Creek and Shoal Creek was selected for the future county seat. They would call it "FAR WEST" as it lay in the western part of the county. In Far West, the Saints built some 200 homes, several dry good stores and groceries, half a dozen blacksmith shops, two hotels, and a printing office. Residents excavated and laid the foundation for a temple and erected a large school building on the town square for use as a courthouse, town hall, and temporary church.

Cooperation and trust replaced the suspicions of the past as relations between the Mormons and Missourians improved remarkably throughout 1837 and early 1838.[4] The Mormon population in Missouri eventually reached 10,000, and Caldwell County became the largest county in western Missouri. By the fall of 1838, Far West was the hub of community activity extending throughout Caldwell, encompassing nearly 2,000 farms over approximately 250,000 acres purchased from the federal government. The rapid influx of Mormons, however, alarmed the older settlers, especially those who had purchased land or town lots in areas they hoped to develop. The developing Mormon enterprises also threatened to displace established merchants and businesses, especially in their trade with Fort Leavenworth. As 1838 wore on, relations between church members and Missouri citizens began a downward spiral. A clash of cultural attitudes set the stage for trouble. Distorted reports and rumors circulated by both camps. Unlawful assemblies of citizens formed on both sides to protect perceived local interests. Some Missourians proposed to drive the Mormons from the state.

Battles ensued, leaving many Mormons dead and wounded eventually leading to Governor Lilburn W. Boggs issuing an order "to exterminate the Mormons, not excepting the women and children, and burn their houses and otherwise destroy their property."[5] The Mormons left peacefully in the bitter cold and winter of 1838 and early 1839, leaving Far West a virtual ghost town. "Beyond the memories, all that physically remains of Far West today are four cornerstones of the envisioned Lord's house or temple at the heart of the former community." The Church of Jesus Christ of Latter-Day Saints (the Mormons) purchased the site and own it today. Markers and cornerstones have been erected there recording its regrettable history.

Caldwell County has had five courthouses, the first being in Far West. In 1843, the county seat was moved to Kingston, which was nearer the center of the population. Thanks to the generosity of two men, James Ramsey and William Hill, who donated 160 acres between them for county purposes.

Today, Caldwell County boasts a population of 9,014 according to a 2015 census. It remains a small, tight-knit, agricultural community and the rural setting, and peaceful, quiet landscape are what keep many generations of families around to call it home.

Endnotes

1. (County Commission of Caldwell County, Missouri 2016)

2. A Brief History of Caldwell County compiled by Charlene Ward

3. The word "hinder" replaced the original text of "retard."

4. John Corrill, A Brief History of the Church of Christ of Latter Day Saints, (Salt Lake City : Modern Microfilm Co., 1970, 1839).

5. History of Caldwell and Livingston counties, Missouri, (St. Louis, Mo. : National Historical Co., 1886)

CHAPTER 14

Camp Names and What's in Them[1]

John Walker Harrington

The following are excerpts taken directly from the 1917 article on the names of the World War I cantonment camps and their namesakes. Prominent in this article was Camp Doniphan in Oklahoma.

Chapter Page Image: A 1917-line drawing from the *Kansas City Star* of the Doniphan Statue in Richmond prior to its installaton. -- A Statue to a Famous Missourian. (1917, January 26). Kansas City Star, p. 7.

The thrill of great deeds of arms is in the names of the 32 cantonments where American men are being trained to follow the traditions of the forefathers, and yet to most of us some of these titles are hardly even reminiscent. Camp Grant tells its own story on an instant. But it requires a quick search of half-forgotten history when we read that one cantonment represents that intrepid leader of mysterious origin who hurled a regiment of Missourians across the then unknown desert of alkali to plant the Stars and Stripes at Sacramento. For the board of which Major Gen. Joseph E. Kuhn was the head selected not only names of men everybody would recognize; they chose some also which would make the nation remember and revive the exploits of neglected worthies.

Prominent officers of past wars, Union and Confederate leaders, are included in the new nomenclature; cognomens duplicated by those well-known men now living were omitted. As far as possible, the name selected for a camp was that of a man from the section typical of the troops there assembled. The effort was made to use names of federal commanders for camps of divisions for the Northern states and of Confederate generals for cantonments where Southern troops had been mobilized. When it was impractical to follow this rule, recourse was had to the index of officers who had served in the American revolution, in the Mexican War of 1846, or in Indian Wars, or to the records of explorers and pioneers.

So it came to pass that the board opened many a cache of glory and has caused many to recall the splendid achievements of leaders whose large part in the making of our national history had not had general public recognition.

Camp Doniphan

Camp Doniphan at Fort Still, Okla., does not instantly suggest to many the career of one of the most remarkable characters in the military annals of the United States—Col. Alexander W. Doniphan. He was supposed to have been of Spanish origin, not Irish, as might be inferred from his name. The name according to tradition, was originally Don Alphonso, and was borne by an ancestor who on account of religious persecutions fled from Spain to England. The cognomen, as many transplanted ones of Latin origin often do, became modified and corrupted in the British home.

Doniphan was practicing law at Liberty, MO., when the call to take up arms against Mexico reached that region in 1846, and Col. Stephen W. Kearny was instructed to move a force to the Pacific coast and seize the Mexican settlements. Owing to dissensions which centered about Gen. Winfield Scott, then at the head of the army of the United States, no adequate plan or preparation was made for the conduct of the war, Kearny did the best he could and pressed westward, followed by fleets of prairie schooners. Doniphan assembled 900 riflemen, known later as the First Missouri cavalry, and conveyed them across the great American desert. Had they not been victors, they would have undoubtedly starved to death.

Doubtless there was never a more quixotic emprise since the beginning of time. In the hands of a leader less romantic and daring, the Doniphan Expedition would have fallen into ruin. Considering the enormous difficulties which beset it, however, it represents one of the greatest feats of American arms, despite the fact that upon this day and generation it has made no great impress. The Mexicans were so confident of capturing the Missourians that they had provided stores of cords and handcuffs in advance with which to bind their captives for a parade in the capital. Doniphan had at the most only 950 half-starved, wild-eyed followers when he attacked 4,200 Mexicans at Sacramento, and scatted them before him. His ragged, unkempt battalions hurled themselves against the enemy with such fury that for years afterwards, the Mexicans spoke of the assault made by the "hairy American devils" who fought like "fiends incarnate."

Doniphan, although he was a man of great personal dignity, especially as one of the leaders of the American bar in the West, had in him the blood of a long line of warrior knights, and fought side by side with his men. His great labor was to hold them in control. The first of the volunteers to leap into the enemy trenches were two raw-boned Missourians, who had a quarrel the day before, which resulted in one of them calling the other a coward. To prove their courage, they ran a race to the Mexican fortifications, scaled the barriers and clubbed many of the foe to death.

Came Out to Fight

On his way to the front, Doniphan encountered one of his command holding seven horses by their bridles, for, as originally planned, 108 men were assigned to this service at the rear.

"Do I have to do this?" exclaimed the dragoon. "Just stand here and hold horses?"

"You do if you have been assigned to it," was the reply.

The man knotted the seven bridles together, threw the knot at the horses' heads, and in a few seconds was running to the front, rifle in hand.

"I came out here to fight," said he. "Hell! I can hold horses in Missouri!"

Doniphan subjugated the fierce Navajo, and established a government over the Mexican settlements, and was in everything the right-hand man of Kearny.

It is especially appropriate that the camp at Linda Vista, Cal., should be named for Brig. Gen. S. W. Kearny, who had so much to do with the conquest of the golden coats. It was his "army of the West," in all only about 2,000 men, which established possession over the whole Pacific slope. With the help of such men as his nephew, Gen. Philip Kearny, and the fearless Doniphan, he was able to wage successful war far from bases of supplies and against tremendous odds. Associated with him was Capt. John C. Fremont for whom is named the camp at Palo Alto, the same gallant soldier and pathfinder who was to become so well known in political circles.

There are further suggestions of the Mexican War in the names of camps which honor the names of Gen. Zachary Taylor and Gen. Pierre G.T. Beauregard, the first at Louisville, KY., and the other at Alexandria, La.

Taken all in all, the titles which have been bestowed on the cantonments of the country bear witness to the many and varied achievements of the officers of the United States.

(Copyright, New York Evening Post, 1917.)

Endnotes

1. ((Harrington 1917)

CHAPTER 15

Sentiments of Honor

Taryn Duffy

A summary of Doniphan's life and how those experiences helped guide some of the significant actions in his life.

Chapter Page Image: One of the last portriats of Alexander W. Doniphan, taken in 1878. -- Garland, R. (1878). Alexander William Doniphan [Three-quarter bust view of General Alexander Doniphan b/w photo]. Retrieved July, 2020, from State Historical Society of Missouri https://digital.shsmo.org/digital/collection/imc/id/22094/rec/1

"It is cold-blooded murder. I will not obey your order...If you execute these men, I will hold you responsible before an earthly tribunal, so help me God."[1] These words were spoken by Alexander William Doniphan, following the Extermination Order issued by Lilburn W. Boggs, a Missouri governor. It is with these words that Doniphan chose to step above what was being asked of him and do what he knew was right. His actions to protect and fight for Joseph Smith Jr. and his followers are his greatest legacy. To understand why Doniphan did what he did, one must first understand who Doniphan was.

Doniphan was born in Mason County, Kentucky to Joseph and Anne Smith Doniphan in 1808. Alexander was the youngest of ten children. Alexander's father served in the Continental Army during the American Revolution and went on to serve as county sheriff and become a prosperous farmer. When Alexander was just five years old, his father died, and Alexander was sent to live with his oldest brother George in Kentucky. At the age of eighteen, he graduated from Augusta College and went on to study law with Martin P. Marshall. Doniphan was able to practice law in Kentucky after being admitted to the bar but decided to seek out other opportunities. By 1830, he moved to Lexington, Missouri, where he gained a reputation as a defense attorney. After living in Lexington, Doniphan moved to Liberty where he became friends with David Rice Atchison, who served as a senator. Doniphan also joined the Liberty Blues. The Liberty Blues was a local militia group. When Doniphan joined this militia, he started his military career.

Because I wish to showcase Doniphan's character using the Missouri Mormon War, which takes place in 1838 but also shows his military career, I am going to skip to the Mexican American War in 1846 and the role he played in that, then conclude with the Missouri Mormon War. Doniphan was requested by Governor John C. Edwards to help raise troops. Doniphan volunteered to fight as a private in Clay County.[2] In November of 1846, Doniphan and his men were ordered into the Navajo territory. Their objective was to overpower and chastise the Navajo. Doniphan and his men had to go through the Rockies, which meant snow and lots of it. Though the trek may have been less than ideal, Doniphan was successful in proctoring a treaty with the Native Americans. After taking time to refresh supplies and his men, they proceeded to go on what has become known as Doniphan's Expedition.[3] The Doniphan Expedition was a march the consisted of about 3,600 miles; this included going through Santa Fe, Chihuahua, Saltillo, and lastly Matamoras. After the war, he continued to practice law.

Doniphan achieved much both in war and outside, but his greatest show of character was seen during the Mormon Missouri War. The Mormon Missouri War was a conflict between the Latter-day Saints and northern Missouri. The war consisted of mob attacks and threats leading to state officials to get involved. It was in the summer of 1838 that the violence and opposition came to a boiling point. The church would no longer stand for the persecution of its people and the denial of their natural rights just as some in Missouri wished for the Mormons to leave. In other words, it was like being stuck between a rock and a hard place. When the election happened, the people of Carroll County voted to cast out the Mormons while surrounding counties voted to stop the Mormons from moving.[4] The Saints asked for protection and some was offered, but when a

Mormon settlement was destroyed, they fled for their lives. When the governor offered no words of wisdom or sorrow, the Saints finally start to fight back. This is when Governor Lilburn W. Boggs issued what became known as Extermination Order.

The words that were meant to put an end to the conflict between the Mormons and Missourians were clear; "Exterminated or driven from the state if necessary."[5] These words show that the Mormons did not equate to the same as everyone else living in the area. They were a threat in the eyes of some. But in the eyes of Alexander Doniphan, they were just people; people who deserved better treatment. Doniphan was given the orders to "take Joseph and the other prisoners into the public square of Far West, and shoot them at 9 o'clock to-morrow morning."[6] As seen at the beginning, Doniphan not only refuses, but also stands up for the rights of these people. Though this marked the end of Smith's hope for a Zion in Missouri, it really helped showcase what kind of man Doniphan was—an honorable one.

Doniphan died on the August 8, 1887. In remembrance of him, a life-sized statue stands in front of the Ray County Courthouse. Doniphan left a legacy of fairness behind from his time as a powerful lawyer and from the great military victories he led. When describing Doniphan's character D.C. Allen says, "By the dead gaze of all of his ancestors; And by the mystery of his Spanish blood, Charged with the awe and glories of the past."[7] What Allen is referencing is how Doniphan seemed to be unable to be anything less than honorable because it goes against not just his own values and morals, but against generations of all Doniphan's that came before him. Alexander William Doniphan can teach us all valuable lessons. If everyone is saying do this, do that, and listen to what you know is right rather then listening to the crowd.

Endnotes

1. Roger Launius, *Alexander William Doniphan* (Columbia, MO: University of Missouri Press, 1997), 219.

2. Dewitt Clinton Allen. *A Sketch of the Life and Character of Col. Alexander W. Doniphan.* Printed at the Advance office, 1897. http://hdl.handle.net/2027/loc.ark:/13960/t3zs35572.

3. Allen, *A Sketch of the Life...*

4. "Mormon-Missouri War of 1838." The Church of Jesus Christ of Latter-day Saints. Accessed December 31, 2019. https://www.churchofjesuschrist.org/study/history/topics/mormon-missouri-war-of-1838?lang=eng.

5. "Extermination Order." The Church of Jesus Christ of Latter-day Saints. Accessed December 31, 2019. https://www.churchofjesuschrist.org/study/history/topics/extermination-order?lang=eng.

6. "Missouri Honors Man Who Refused Order to Kill the Prophet Joseph Smith." The Church of Jesus Christ of Latter-day Saints. Accessed December 31, 2019. https://www.churchofjesuschrist.org/study/ensign/1995/01/news-of-the-church/missouri-honors-man-who-refused-order-to-kill-the-prophet-joseph-smith?lang=eng.

7. Allen, *A Sketch of the Life...*

Bibliography

Allen, Dewitt Clinton. *A Sketch of the Life and Character of Col. Alexander W. Doniphan.*
    Printed at the Advance office,, 1897. http://hdl.handle.net/2027/loc.ark:/13960/t3zs35572.

"Extermination Order." The Church of Jesus Christ of Latter-day Saints. Accessed December 31, 2019. https://www.churchofjesuschrist.org/study/history/topics/extermination-order?lang=eng.

"Missouri Honors Man Who Refused Order to Kill the Prophet Joseph Smith." The Church of Jesus Christ of Latter-day Saints. Accessed December 31, 2019. https://www.churchofjesuschrist.org/study/ensign/1995/01/news-of-the-church/missouri-honors-man-who-refused-order-to-kill-the-prophet-joseph-smith?lang=eng.

"Mormon-Missouri War of 1838." The Church of Jesus Christ of Latter-day Saints. Accessed December 31, 2019. https://www.churchofjesuschrist.org/study/history/topics/mormon-missouri-war-of-1838?lang=eng.

Roger Launius, *Alexander William Doniphan* Columbia, MO: University of Missouri press, 1997,

Hubbell & Doniphan House

Hicks Photo Collection

Doniphan - Hubbell House

From circa 1830 until 1925 a house stood on this site once occupied by Alexander W. Doniphan. A native Kentuckian, Doniphan practiced law in Clay County for 30 years, defended the Mormons, and founded William Jewell College. During the Mexican War in 1846 - 47, he commanded the First Regiment Missouri Mounted Volunteers in the longest march ever made by an American military organization. During this expedition, he became known as "The Hero of Sacramento." The house was occupied at other times by Peter H. Burnett, first governor of California, and for many years the Hubbell family.

CHAPTER 16

Alexander Doniphan Marches to Truman Library

John Dillingham, May 17, 2007

This was the introduction to a speech on Alexander W. Doniphan given by John Dillingham to the Civil War Roundtable of Western Missouri, at the Harry S. Truman Presidential Library.

Chapter Page Image: Doniphan - Hubbell House and historical marker where the house once stood. -- *Photo Courtesy of Clay County Museum, Liberty, Missouri and Giving River Images/Valerie Anderson.*

It's only right that John Dillingham's talk on "Alexander Doniphan, Citizen Soldier" should be given at the Truman Library on May 17, 2007 at 7 p.m. After all, Harry Truman trained at Camp Doniphan in Oklahoma. Dillingham is no stranger to the Truman Library since he used the Library's resources to write his master's thesis on the 1948 Whistle Stop Campaign. He also had a 45-minute interview with President Truman who said, "Oh, yes, that's the election I was supposed to lose."

In the University Press of Kansas book, Doniphan's Epic March, the First Missouri Volunteers in the Mexican War by Joseph G. Dawson III, the reviewer says that between 1846 and 1847, a ragtag army of 800 American[1] volunteers marched 3,500 miles across deserts and mountains, through Native American[1] territory and into Mexico. There they handed the Mexican army one of its most demoralizing defeats and helped the U.S. win its first foreign war. Their leader was Alexander Doniphan, a Liberty, Missouri lawyer, later became a national hero of the Mexican-American War.

Doniphan is also known for his role in Mormon history when as a brigadier general in the state militia, he arrested the prophet Joseph Smith Jr. and other leaders, forcing them to leave Missouri. He refused to follow orders to execute Smith and prevented vigilantes from harming him.

As a civilian, Doniphan opposed secession and favored neutrality for Missouri. Although he was offered high command by the Union, he did not take an active part in the Civil War. In the late 1860s, he established his law office in Richmond, Missouri and ran a bank until his death in 1887. He is buried in Fairview Cemetery in Liberty under an obelisk.

Also, as a civilian, Alexander Doniphan was a strong supporter of education and served as Clay County's first school commissioner in 1853 and was instrumental in securing William Jewell College for Liberty. Even today the Alexander Doniphan Heritage Society recognizes those who make significant contributions to the college. In 1909, the Alexander Doniphan Chapter of the Daughters of the American Revolution was formed in Liberty.

"Doniphan sightings" can be found in street names in Liberty and at Fort Leavenworth, Kansas where he is in the Hall of Fame. In 1918, the State of Missouri dedicated a magnificent monument of bronze and granite at Richmond, Missouri, in his memory.

More recently, John Dillingham was instrumental in getting Missouri Highway 152 in Clay and Platte County named for Alexander Doniphan, and he would like to see him included in the Hall of Famous Missourians at the State Capitol in Jefferson City.

Among those in favor would surely be the citizens of Doniphan, Missouri, near Poplar Bluff in Ripley County. The curator of the Current River Heritage Museum, Lynn Maples, recounts that the town was named for Alexander Doniphan because the son of a town father had fought with him and admired him greatly. In the account of General Sterling W. Price's invasion of Missouri in October of 1864, which ended at the Battle of Westport in Kansas City, it is said that he led 12,000 Confederate cavalrymen from Arkansas into Missouri near Doniphan.

In 1965, General Alexander Doniphan was featured in television's "Profiles in Courage" and was played by Peter Lawford, the brother-in-law of President John F. Kennedy.

Doniphan distinguished himself not only by leading one of the most notable military marches of all time during the Mexican War, but also for helping keep Missouri in the Union during the Civil War.

John Dillingham shows a great love of the history of the Northland by serving as the president of the Clay County Historical Board and the Northland Betterment Committee, but he has spent many volunteer hours south of the Missouri River as well especially in his high-profile service as president of the Liberty Memorial Association, which recently opened the National World War I Museum. He has also served as a member of the Kansas City Police Board and is a director of the Command and General Staff College Foundation at Fort Leavenworth, Kansas. Dillingham is a former president of the Native Sons and Daughters of Kansas City.

Dillingham's talk on "Alexander Doniphan, Citizen Soldier" is presented by the Civil War Round Table of Western Missouri in cooperation with the Truman Presidential Museum and Library, this year celebrating its fiftieth anniversary. The Library is located at 500 West U.S. 24 Highway in Independence, Missouri. The talk is free with a paid admission to the Library of $7 regular admission, $5-seniors, $3-children 6-18 years, and free for children under 6.

The Truman Museum will be open from 9 a.m. to 9 p.m. on Thursday, May 17, and you are invited to tour the permanent exhibits plus the special showing of "Treasures of the Presidents," which highlights the historical collections of the nation's presidential libraries. On display will be ornate gifts from heads-of-state, simple handmade tokens of appreciation from ordinary people, documents that shaped the course of history, personal letters from the presidents, and audio and video recordings.

Endnotes

1. Text originally used "Indian" instead of "Native American."

CHAPTER 17

Civil War Roundtable: Alexander W. Doniphan

John Dillingham, May 17, 2007
at the Harry S. Truman Presidential Library

*John Dillingham's speech about Alexander Doniphan.
at the Harry S. Truman Presidential Library.*

Chapter Page Image: Plaque on the Alexander W. Doniphan Statue in Richmond, Missouri. -- *Anderson, Valerie. (2020, April 29). Doniphan Statue at the Ray County Courthouse [Photograph]. Giving River Images, Richmond, MO.*

Thank you for the opportunity and honor to be here tonight as a guest of the Civil War Roundtable of Western Missouri and for, perhaps, a first-time meeting at the Truman Library. Mike Calvert, as President, you're very fortunate to have Beverly Shaw. Her follow-through for months has been tremendous.

Tonight, we're going to introduce some of you for the first time to Alexander W. Doniphan, known by his friends and family as Will. To us, he is a citizen soldier, a lawyer, an orator, a legislator, and educator; but to members of The Church of Jesus Christ of Latter-day Saints, he is a Savior. Who is Doniphan? Why would I, from Clay County, be asked to speak on this man born 200 years ago next year?

If you believe in fate, or are curious about unusual situations, may I submit the following to set tonight's stage:

Doniphan's father was Joseph Doniphan, first teacher at Boonesborough, where my dad's third great-grandfather enabled me to be a member of that society—both there at the same time on the Kentucky River below Lexington.

Recently, I visited Doniphan's obelisk in Fairview Cemetery, Liberty, where to my surprise, I find in the adjoining family plot, my great-grandfather's close friend, Civil War Regimental Surgeon Doctor John Marshall Allen, whose name our family now carries. His brother D.C. Allen was Doniphan's close friend.

As I stood on the Missouri Speaker of the House's dais several weeks ago in Jefferson City, I reflected on the fact that in an earlier Capitol building in 1858, my great-great-grandfather—

waiting for a national civil war to break out, fueled by our border wars—served from Clay County in a seat occupied by Doniphan three years earlier. They had to have known each other.

Lastly, speaking here tonight, the coincidence that Doniphan's grandfather was also Alexander, perhaps the namesake, born in 1716, died in 1768 in Stafford, Virginia. He had a younger brother named Anderson Doniphan. Their father was Mott Doniphan, who was Alexander W. Doniphan's great-grandfather and Harry S. Truman's fourth great-grandfather. So, standing on this stage, the week after the President's 123rd birthday, is it fate that this first-ever meeting is featuring a distant cousin?

Our friend, Congressman Ike Skelton likes to remind me that Doniphan was admitted to the Lafayette County Bar in 1830. There is a bronze, granite historical marker to this effect next to the street on the site of the old courthouse in Lexington, east of the current downtown. In 1833, he moved to Liberty to join David Rice Atchison, later first Circuit Judge of the New Platte Purchase, first U.S. Senator from western Missouri, and Acting President of the United States for one day. I understand Peter Burnett was a member of the firm or very close. He would later become the first governor of California. Not too shabby for a law firm, north of the Missouri River.

Again, who is Doniphan? Where does one start for a man who died when Harry Truman was three? Missouri boasts of some thirty generals with a strong connection to our state, a majority during the Civil War. What if I told you the Dictionary of Missouri Biography, and a recent book by the University of Missouri Press, lists the most famous as Alexander "Will" Doniphan, Governor Sterling W. Price, President Ulysses S. Grant,

John J. Pershing, and Omar N. Bradley. From the Mexican War to World War II—not bad company!

Missouri Life said, "In his era, he was a superstar." Doniphan led about 800 ragtag Clay/Platte men on a 3,500-plus mile land trek and another 1,000 by water, the First Missouri Mounted Volunteer Regiment, to victory in the Mexican War from 1846 to 1847. Rumor has it he read books on infantry tactics and on how to be a general, borrowed from his commander, during his trip south. Remember, he was an attorney, not a West Pointer.

He defeated larger Mexican forces at El Brazito and Sacramento and occupied Santa Fe, El Paso del Norte, and Chihuahua. Always the lawyer, he led the committee, during a month-long stay in Santa Fe, that created a new government for the New Mexico Territory by melding legal concepts of Spanish, Mexican, and U.S. law to create a new code which, I understand, is the foundation of today's New Mexico Constitution. He also helped pave the way for the annexation of the territory that became New Mexico and Arizona. All in one year!

For those heroic military efforts, since the troops assembled and left from our neighbor Fort Leavenworth, Kansas, General Doniphan hangs in Fort Leavenworth's Hall of Fame, along with our Nation's greatest; this for leading the longest march in U.S. military history. This includes being next to my friend Colonel Roger Donlan, the first Medal of Honor recipient in Vietnam, who lives at Leavenworth.

On a lighter note, I learned that on Doniphan's victorious return, Major John Dougherty provided from Multnomah, on the location today of the new Staley Farm Development, two buffalo

THE WILL OF MISSOURI: THE LIFE, TIMES, & INFLUENCE OF ALEXANDER WILLIAM DONIPHAN

for a big barbecue. I called my friend Ollie Gates, upon learning this important news, to suggest the first barbecue in Kansas City, was in the Northland.

His reputation as a leader formed back in the 1830's. While in his late twenties, he served on the committee that later saw Congressional approval of the Platte Purchase, adding six counties west and north of Clay County to the Missouri River. I've heard it's the only time in U.S. history where Congress added onto a state. In addition, Doniphan played an important state ratifying role as a freshman member of the Missouri General Assembly in 1836.

I understand his early legal work, since Atchison was occupied, was in Jackson County, on the so-called Mormon problems. I'd like to interject that Missouri Governor Boggs issued the infamous Extermination Order of all Mormons in 1838 and not until 1976 under Governor Kit Bond was it lifted. I told my friend Tony Sarver that here in Missouri, it was legally open season for 136 years. In their later years, Doniphan and Atchison both competed for the U.S. Senate at the Lexington Convention as Whigs and Democrats. But, as twenty-five-year-olds, they hunted and fished together, gambled in taverns with friends, and saw each other in court.

Atchison organized a Liberty Blues militia company. Doniphan became an officer as well. Apparently they "drilled three times per year, marched around in the sun for a while and then settled down for a picnic and not just a little drink," according to one source.

One observation, if successful in a parallel to the removal of Native American[1] tribes of Platte, a so-called Mormon Reservation would be created, and Platte would be free for non-Mormon settlement. Doniphan recalled later that the Mormons broke their agreement and formed a settlement in Daviess County. Reportedly, there were 10,000 Mormons in 1838 in this area—a very large population at that time.

Atchison, now commanding general in northwest Missouri, called out 400 Clay or Platte County men to quell disturbances in Daviess County. Clay County Commander Doniphan was sent to Caldwell County to secure Mormon prisoners' release. Following a "friendly chat" with Joseph Smith Jr., the Mormon Prophet, and success, he also secured releases in Daviess County. Both men were retained by the Mormons for assistance in their Jackson County troubles. With their lands taken and followers forcibly driven out, Doniphan led an effort of compromise. As Captain of the aforementioned Liberty Blues, he provided court appearance and physical protection for the Saints. Even though only partially successful, he was approved and hired again after the Mormon War of 1838.

When Mormons came to Clay from Jackson County in 1834, Doniphan spoke for reason against mob violence. He later joined with Atchison asking the Mormons to leave Clay County to avoid civil strife. In 1836 in the Missouri General Assembly, Doniphan introduced a bill organizing Caldwell County out of northern Ray County, as a place for the Mormons to live. "All was quiet for a few months" according to [Stephen C.] LeSueur in The Mormon War.

In the fall, as Mormon soldiers prepared to march, Doniphan rode to Far West with sixty men, but his advice for calm was not followed. Governor Boggs mobilized the state militia, replaced

Atchison with Samuel Lucas and ordered the Mormons to be exterminated. Doniphan prevented Missouri soldiers from shooting Mormon prisoners. A kangaroo "court martial" ordered execution of Joseph Smith Jr. and other leaders and General Lucas ordered now Brigadier General Doniphan, of the mobilized state militia, to carry out the order at 9 a.m. the next morning. Doniphan, answered by note, "it is coldblooded murder. I will not obey your order. My brigade shall march for Liberty tomorrow morning at 8 o'clock; and if you execute these men, I will hold you responsible before an earthly tribunal, so help me God!"

I have to add some personal levity; it's a real conflict of interest asking a lawyer to execute his client. Today the historic Liberty Jail in Liberty is a shrine operated by the Latter-day Saints that tells the story of Joseph Smith and five Mormon leaders who were saved because Doniphan refused a direct order to execute these leaders. I think one can safely say the church was saved for the worldwide mission we see today. Not only the LDS, but also here in Independence with the Community of Christ church.[2] Several revelations from Joseph Smith occurred while imprisoned in Liberty before his so-called escape and journey to Nauvoo, Illinois.

It was an honor and inspiration for me several years ago to receive the Doniphan Award on a small stage that serves as the roof to that small jail that was so significant from 1838 to 1839. I'm pleased to announce that a longtime Liberty Councilwoman and educator will receive the Doniphan Award this Saturday night, Juarenne Hester, to strains of the Doniphan March. President John F. Kennedy did a profile in courage on Doniphan, highlighting this significant time that perhaps saved the Mormon Church. Peter Lawford, President Kennedy's brother-in-law, portrayed Doniphan in a movie.

When our fourteen-month effort asking the Missouri Department of Transportation to name Missouri Highway 152 in honor of Alexander Doniphan in Clay and Platte Counties was successful, we broke with tradition and had the ceremony in Liberty at the Alexander Doniphan Elementary School. Five students enacted five different facets of his life while retired Circuit Judge Ken Elliott with that deep baritone voice portrayed, in top hat and coat, his hero, Doniphan. As he appeared from the back he said, "Thank you boys and girls for remembering this old soldier."

Doniphan Highway parallels the military road, begun in 1827, in the area that later would become Platte County. It was built by soldiers, and ran from Fort Leavenworth to Barry, which today is on the Clay-Platte County line, but was originally the former state line. Settlers built the Clay County portion from Barry to Liberty, where the main street leading to the square is called Kansas. In 1827, Liberty was the Quick Trip of the day for families of the Fort, both for physical and social needs.

The school on the hill is there because of Founder Trustee Alexander Doniphan. William Jewell College was created in 1849. The Baptists wanted Boonville, but Doniphan had raised the money and suggested noted Columbia educator Dr. William Jewell, to be the first President of the school that would carry his name. Doniphan was successful and, ironically, was a Disciple of Christ, not Baptist.

I earlier had mentioned Doniphan's father Joseph was the first teacher at Fort Boonesborough, Kentucky. Alexander Doniphan served as Clay County's first Commissioner of Education. He served three terms in the Missouri House, in

1836, 1840 and 1854. Today, there is a Doniphan Society at William Jewell; a leadership institute for the Clay County Economic Development Council; a town named for him in Ripley County; a county in Kansas; and a road in El Paso, Texas and Liberty, Missouri.

Today, the Clay County Commission and the Clay County Millennium Historic Board are completing the fundraising necessary to place Alexander W. Doniphan in the Hall of Famous Missourians, close to his old partner David Rice Atchison. Missouri Speaker of the House, Rod Jetton, has been most supportive in this effort.

If the Civil War had not come along, Doniphan probably would be a person of national prominence. However, when he turned down a high command during the Civil Way and left the area to practice law and relocate in St. Louis, he fell from sight. His commitment to the Union prohibited him from taking up arms against it, and his allegiance to friends and institutions of the South prevented him from aiding in the putting down of the rebellion. In the end, he served as a state claims agent for the widows and orphans of killed soldiers.

After the war, he reestablished his law offices in Richmond, Missouri where he died. He was a Union man, who early had slaves, who believed in preserving the Union and favored neutrality for Missouri in 1861 and served as a delegate to the Washington Peace Conference, where President-elect Abraham Lincoln observed "and this is Colonel Doniphan who made the wild march against the Navajos and Mexicans," he added, "You are the only man I ever met who in appearance came up to my previous expectation." He was six-foot-four, muscular, imposing, with a shock of thick auburn hair.

In 1909, a chapter of the Daughters of the American Revolution was named in his honor and organized in Liberty. In 1918, the State of Missouri dedicated a magnificent monument of bronze and granite at Richmond, in Ray County to his memory. In 1998, Roger Launius, Chief Historian for NASA, wrote Alexander William Doniphan: Portrait of a Missouri Moderate. Governor Mel Carnahan proclaimed Alexander Doniphan Day in Missouri on October 24, 1994, apparently on extermination day, 156 years later. I suggested recently to the Mormon Church that the sacred site of Far West, where the cornerstones for the Temple were laid, before Salt Lake became their home, that crowded Brigham Young University consider an eastern campus carrying the name of Alexander Doniphan University.

"The moderation that Doniphan's life represented," according to Launius, "speaks to the present crisis in American politics. As extreme positions seem increasingly to be advanced, less and less room in the middle for interchange and compromise seems possible. Doniphan was appalled by similar development in the 1850s and 1860s, and his perspective might instruct Americans today....Doniphan's career provides a useful means of exploring past perspectives and political situations." As Launius observes, "his life may help provide information useful in developing a paradigm shift for present action, for clearly many of the general problems and issues with which he dealt have resurfaced in a variety of ways since his time."

As you can tell, 120 years after the death of Alexander W. Doniphan, I think we can say, "he's gone but not forgotten." I hope you have enjoyed learning a little more about Mr. Truman's cousin, Will Doniphan of Clay County. I think they would be pleased and proud of each other.

Thank you all for being here tonight.

Endnotes

1. The term "Native Americans" replaced the original text of "Indian."

2. The speech initially referenced "RLDS" instead of "Community of Christ." The Latter-day Saints denomination now known as the "Community of Christ" were named the "Reorganized Church of Jesus Christ of Latter-day Saints" and abbreviated as "RLDS" from 1872 to 2001.

CHAPTER 18

Alexander Doniphan— A Path to Follow

Dr. W. Christian Sizemore

The following remarks were given at the Alexander W. Doniphan Bicentennial Celebration held July 9, 2008, at William Jewell College, Liberty, Missouri, commemorating the 200th anniversary of Doniphan's birth (1808–2008). Dr. Sizemore is the past president (1994–2000) and chancellor (2000–2002) of William Jewell College.

Chapter Page Image: Plaque on the Alexander W. Doniphan Statue in Richmond, MO.
-- Anderson, Valerie. (2020, April 29). Doniphan Statue at the Ray County Courthouse [Photograph]. Giving River Images, Richmond, MO.

The Alexander W. Doniphan Bicentennial Celebration in Liberty, Missouri, on July 9, 2008, was a celebration of leadership. But what is leadership? Is it intelligence, ability, strength, station in life, being in the right place at the right time, or who you know?

In 1961, the U.S. had four Nobel Prize winners. President John F. Kennedy welcomed these four distinguished leaders to the White House with this observation, "I think this is the most extraordinary collection of talent, of human knowledge, that has ever been gathered together at the White House, with the possible exception of when Thomas Jefferson dined alone." (Kennedy 1962)

Jefferson was truly a Renaissance Man, and another Renaissance Man, Alexander William Doniphan, was born during Jefferson's presidency. Doniphan, who lived and worked right here in Liberty, became the Renaissance Man of the western frontier.

At age fourteen, Doniphan enrolled in Augusta College in his native Kentucky. He graduated at age eighteen and spent the next six months on his own studying ancient and modern English literature before reading law. Doniphan was admitted to the bar in Kentucky and Ohio at age twenty. Two years later, he was admitted to the bar in Missouri.

Possessing one of the greatest characteristics of leadership, Doniphan never stopped learning, and he was a voracious reader. Enlisting as a private in the Mexican-American War, Doniphan was elected Colonel of the First Missouri Mounted Volunteer Regiment. On that long march into Mexico, Doniphan, who had never led soldiers in combat, continued to read, studying classical military tactics. Today, West Point cadets study Doniphan's tactics.

Vision is another great leadership characteristic, and Alexander Doniphan was a visionary leader in every area he touched. In the area of education, his leadership began in his own home where he taught his two sons to read, write, and speak French, Spanish, German, and Italian. He was the first Commissioner of Education in Clay County, and under his leadership the first school building in this county was constructed. Doniphan was a founding trustee of William Jewell College, and he personally raised the initial funds to locate the college in Liberty. He literally got on his horse and visiting area residents sold 625 shares in this proposed new venture that would become William Jewell College. The result was a million dollars in present value to form the financial foundation of this new college on the western frontier in 1849.

Doniphan's vision for the military took him through the ranks from private, to colonel, to general, with eventual service on the Board of Visitors of the United States Military Academy at West Point.

In the arena of the law, Doniphan was one of the best trial lawyers of his day. U.S. Senator David Rice Atchison said of Doniphan, "I knew all the great men of country in the earlier days—Clay, Webster, Calhoun, John Quincy Adams, Clayton, Crittenden, and others." But of Doniphan's courtroom oratorical skills, Atchison said, "I heard him climb higher than any of them." (Elliott 1969) Doniphan also wrote the code of civil laws that forms the basis of the current constitution of the state of New Mexico.

In the area of politics, Doniphan served three terms in the Missouri House of Representatives.

In banking and business, Doniphan founded and was president of the bank in Richmond, Missouri.

Doniphan's vision was especially prescient in the area of economic development, for he was responsible for and planned the development of the Platte Purchase that added six counties to the state of Missouri, including all of the territory from Platte County to St. Joseph.

In the area of community service, Doniphan's vision for the future of Liberty was farsighted, for when he arrived in the village of Liberty, there were only 300 inhabitants. But Doniphan saw a vision for what it could become, and he helped develop the business and social structure of Liberty.

Doniphan's primary leadership characteristic was best described by his friend and Liberty attorney, D.C. Allen, who said of Doniphan, "I never knew of anyone whose perception of right and wrong was so strong." (Allen, St. Joseph Gazette, 1887 1997) Doniphan's willingness to take a strong stand is evidenced by his refusal to execute Mormon leader Joseph Smith and his passionate voice on behalf of the preservation of the Union.

In December of 1860 when word of the secession of South Carolina reached Liberty, Doniphan had handbills printed at his own expense and distributed throughout the region. Six thousand citizens responded, gathered on the Courthouse square in Liberty, and stood in the snow listening to Doniphan as he spoke for three hours without notes on the importance of preserving the Union.

Doniphan's strong leadership was recognized beyond the borders of Liberty, Clay County, and Missouri, by none other than President

Abraham Lincoln who appointed Doniphan to the Peace Commission in 1861. Lincoln recognized Doniphan's leadership abilities and described him in these words, "You are the only man I ever met who in appearance came up to my previous expectation." (Allen, "Colonel Alexander W. Doniphan—His Life and Character" 1907)

So we see that leadership is definitely much more than native ability or intelligence, or strength or being in the right place at the right time, or even who you know. Leadership combines character, vision, and service. A leader leaves a path to follow.

Alexander William Doniphan left a path to follow, and it is obvious that Doniphan's qualities of leadership are worthy of our emulation. May we all strive to follow in the footsteps of Alexander Doniphan, so that we, too, will leave a path to follow.

Endnotes

Allen, D.C. "Colonel Alexander W. Doniphan—His Life and Character." In *Doniphan's Expedition, and the Conquest of New Mexico and California,* edited by William Elsey Connelley (Topeka: Crane and Co., 1907), 39.

Allen, D.C. "St. Joseph Gazette, 1887." In *Alexander William Doniphan: Portrait of a Missouri Moderate,* edited by Roger D. Launius, 280. Columbia: University of Missouri Press, 1997.

Elliott, R. Kenneth. "The Rhetoric of Alexander W. Doniphan." *The Trail Guide,* December 1969: 12. Kennedy, John F. *Public Papers of the Presidents.* Washington: American Presidency Project, 1962.

Originally published: Mormon Historical Studies, Vol. 9. No. 2, Fall 2008; revised November, 2019.

Epilogue

Jeremiah Morgan and Steven V. Potter

As we concluded this project in the spring of 2020, our nation has experienced another movement calling for action against the institutional racism that was begat by what many have called America's "original sin" of slavery. Looking at a prominent person of the antebellum period naturally leads to several important questions. Did this person enslave others? What was this person's view on slavery? Can you view nineteenth century actors through a twenty-first century perspective? All these questions come to mind when considering Alexander W. Doniphan.

It is clearly recorded that Doniphan enslaved people. It can also be suggested that Doniphan favored the expansion of slavery at least into the 1850s as he supported opening Kansas for slave-holding Missourians to settle. Despite these positions, it is also clearly recorded that Doniphan was an anti-secessionist and attended the Washington Peace Conference as a last-ditch effort to save the Union. Author and historian, Roger Launius posed the question, "I was asked to speculate on what I would ask Alexander Doniphan if I were ever to meet him. I responded that I would like to ask him how a pro-Union constitutionalist, committed to the rule of law and justice for all, could support the institution of slavery? I'm sure Doniphan labored over this difficult question."

We know that people of that era could change their minds when it came to slavery. Perhaps one of the clearest indications of this kind of evolution can be found in the following well-known quotation. It was written by another former Whig party politician like Doniphan. In 1862, less than a year before the Emancipation Proclamation, Abraham Lincoln penned, "If I could save the Union without freeing any slave I would do it, and if I could save it by freeing all the slaves I would do it; and if I could save it by freeing some and leaving others alone I would also do that." This position does not sound particularly enlightened in the twenty-first century context. Furthermore, the statement seems to indicate that Lincoln himself was willing to sustain institutional racism and continue to enslave people if it meant the Union would be preserved. If this was once the position of The Great Emancipator, could anyone from the antebellum period be "acceptable" from a modern perspective?

As you have seen, there is a courthouse statue of Doniphan. There is a school as well as places and streets honoring Doniphan. There was also a military camp named for Doniphan. Should all these honors and memorials be removed given what little we know and what we can presume about Doniphan's views on race? History is not learned through memorials. It is learned through stories, archives, and records. The previous essays tell a lot about Doniphan and the great acts of his life. There is not much recorded about Doniphan and his views on slavery compared to several of his contemporaries. It can certainly be argued that, many people living between the 1840s and the 1880s had evolving attitudes and perceptions about the institution of slavery. It can also be easily concluded that even the most enlightened people of that time would not be considered so today.

There is no way to deny that the American experience and culture is greatly influenced by our "original sin" and the institutional racism that followed. There are many examples that show that Doniphan was exceptionally committed to the rule of law. We want to believe that if he were alive today, Doniphan would support laws and regulations that provide equal footing, equal treatment, and equal rights for all. However, this opinion is only projection, an assumption, and cannot be proven. Racism embraced by or endorsed through norms, values, and especially codified in law or government practice is wrong. When such situations are uncovered, we should work with all haste to eliminate them. We understand that today, and we want to believe that Doniphan would understand that, too.

Image Gallery

Figure 1: Alexander W. Doniphan found in the centennial work, Missouri's Hall of Fame. This is the full version of this image found earlier in this book.

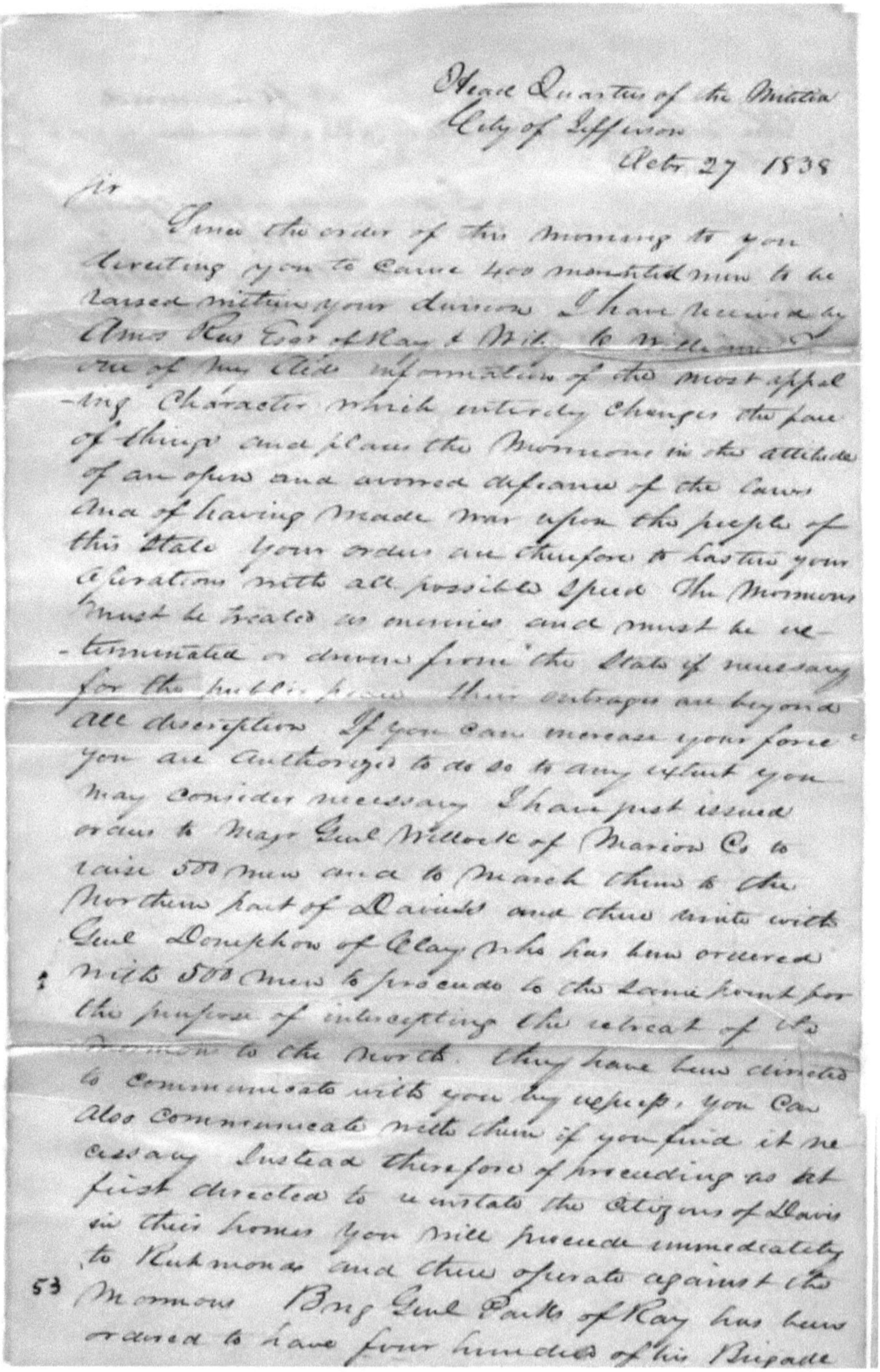
Head Quarters of the Militia
City of Jefferson
Octr 27 1838

Sir

Since the order of this morning to you
directing you to cause 400 mounted men to be
raised within your division I have received by
Amos Rees Esqr of Ray & Wiley C Williams Esqr
one of my Aids information of the most appal
-ing Character which entirely changes the face
of things and places the Mormons in the attitude
of an open and avowed defiance of the laws
and of having made war upon the people of
this State Your orders are therefore to hasten your
operations with all possible speed The Mormons
must be treated as enemies and must be ex
-terminated or driven from the State if necessary
for the public peace their outrages are beyond
all description If you can increase your force
you are authorized to do so to any extent you
may consider necessary I have just issued
orders to Major Genl Willock of Marion Co to
raise 500 men and to march them to the
Northern part of Daviess and there unite with
Genl Doniphan of Clay who has been ordered
with 500 men to proceed to the same point for
the purpose of intercepting the retreat of the
Mormons to the north. they have been directed
to communicate with you by express, you can
also communicate with them if you find it ne
cessary Instead therefore of proceeding as at
first directed to reinstate the citizens of Daviess
in their homes you will proceed immediately
to Richmond and there operate against the
53 Mormons Brig Genl Parks of Ray has been
ordered to have four hundred of his Brigade

Figure 2: Governor Lilburn Boggs order to expel (or "exterminate if necessary") the Latter-day Saints from Missouri. This is the full version of this image found earlier in this book.

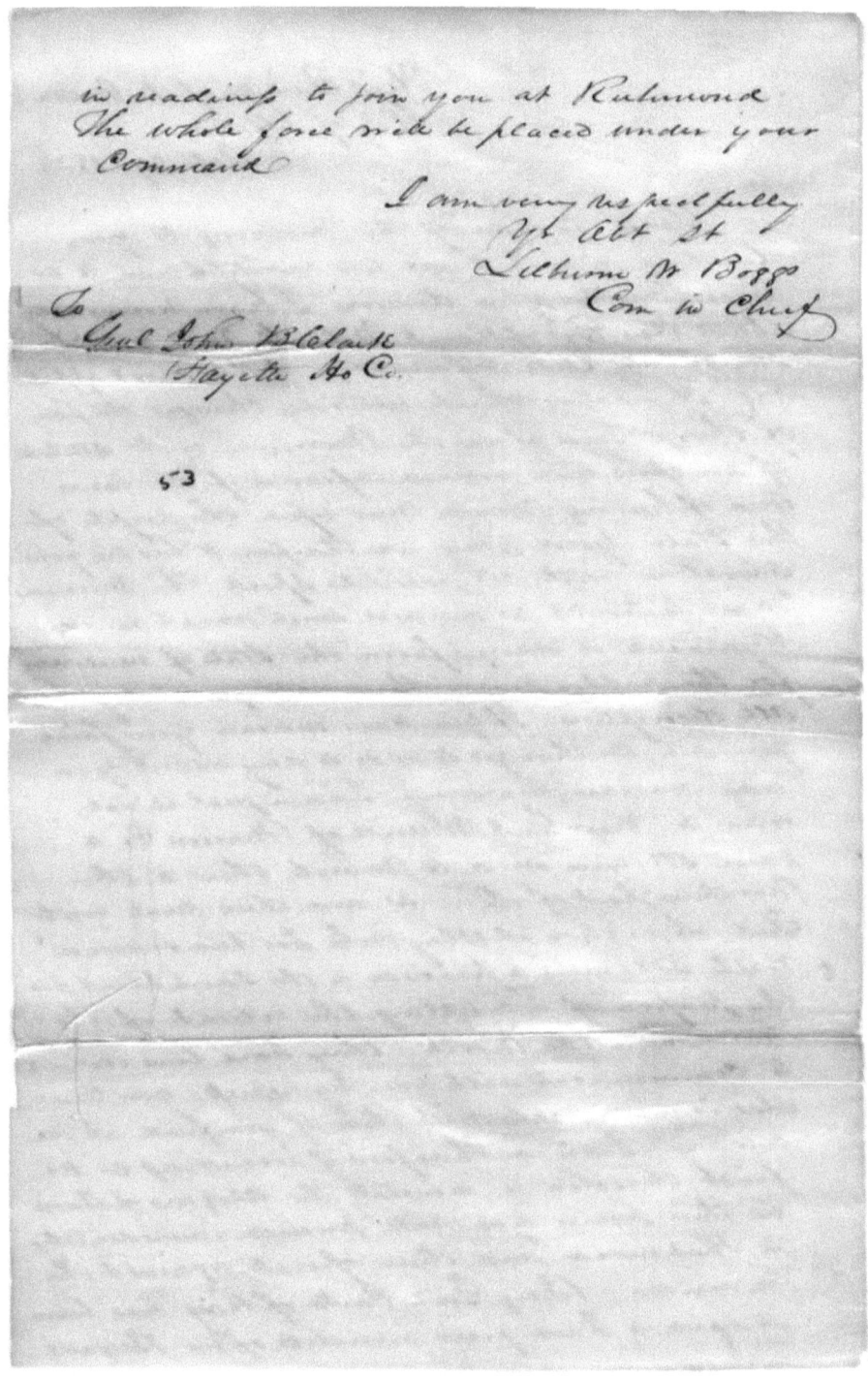

Figure 3: Governor Lilburn Boggs order to expel (or "exterminate if necessary") the Latter-day Saints from Missouri. This is the full version of this image found earlier in this book.

CHRISTOPHER S. BOND
GOVERNOR

EXECUTIVE OFFICE
STATE OF MISSOURI
JEFFERSON CITY

FILED
JUN 2 5 1976

SECRETARY OF STATE

EXECUTIVE ORDER

WHEREAS, on October 27, 1838, the Governor of the State of Missouri, Lilburn W. Boggs, issued an order calling for the extermination or expulsion of Mormons from the State of Missouri; and

WHEREAS, Governor Boggs' order clearly contravened the rights to life, liberty, property and religious freedom as guaranteed by the Constitution of the United States, as well as the Constitution of the State of Missouri; and

WHEREAS, in this Bicentennial year as we reflect on our nation's heritage, the exercise of religious freedom is without question one of the basic tenets of our free democratic republic;

NOW, THEREFORE, I, CHRISTOPHER S. BOND, Governor of the State of Missouri, by virtue of the authority vested in me by the Constitution and the laws of the State of Missouri, do hereby order as follows:

> Expressing on behalf of all Missourians our deep regret for the injustice and undue suffering which was caused by this 1838 order, I hereby rescind Executive Order Number 44 dated October 27, 1838, issued by Governor Lilburn W. Boggs.

Figure 4: Governor Bond's rescission of the Boggs extermination order

Page 2

IN WITNESS WHEREOF: I have hereunto set my hand and
caused to be affixed the great
seal of the State of Missouri in
the City of Jefferson on this
25th day of June, 1976.

GOVERNOR

ATTEST

SECRETARY OF STATE

Figure 5: Governor Bond's rescission of the Boggs extermination order

Figure 6: Missouri's Mounted Volunteers led by Doniphan in a highly stylized lithograph depicting the Battle of Sacramento. This is the full version of this image found earlier in this book.

Figure 7: Portraits taken in 1888 of the surviving members of Captain A.P. Moss' (2) Company serving under Doniphan (1) in the Mexican War. This is the full version of this image found earlier in this book.

Figure 8: Sheet music for "Col. Doniphan's Grand March." Figure 8 is the full version of this image found earlier in this book.

Figure 9: Sheet music for "Col. Doniphan's Grand March."

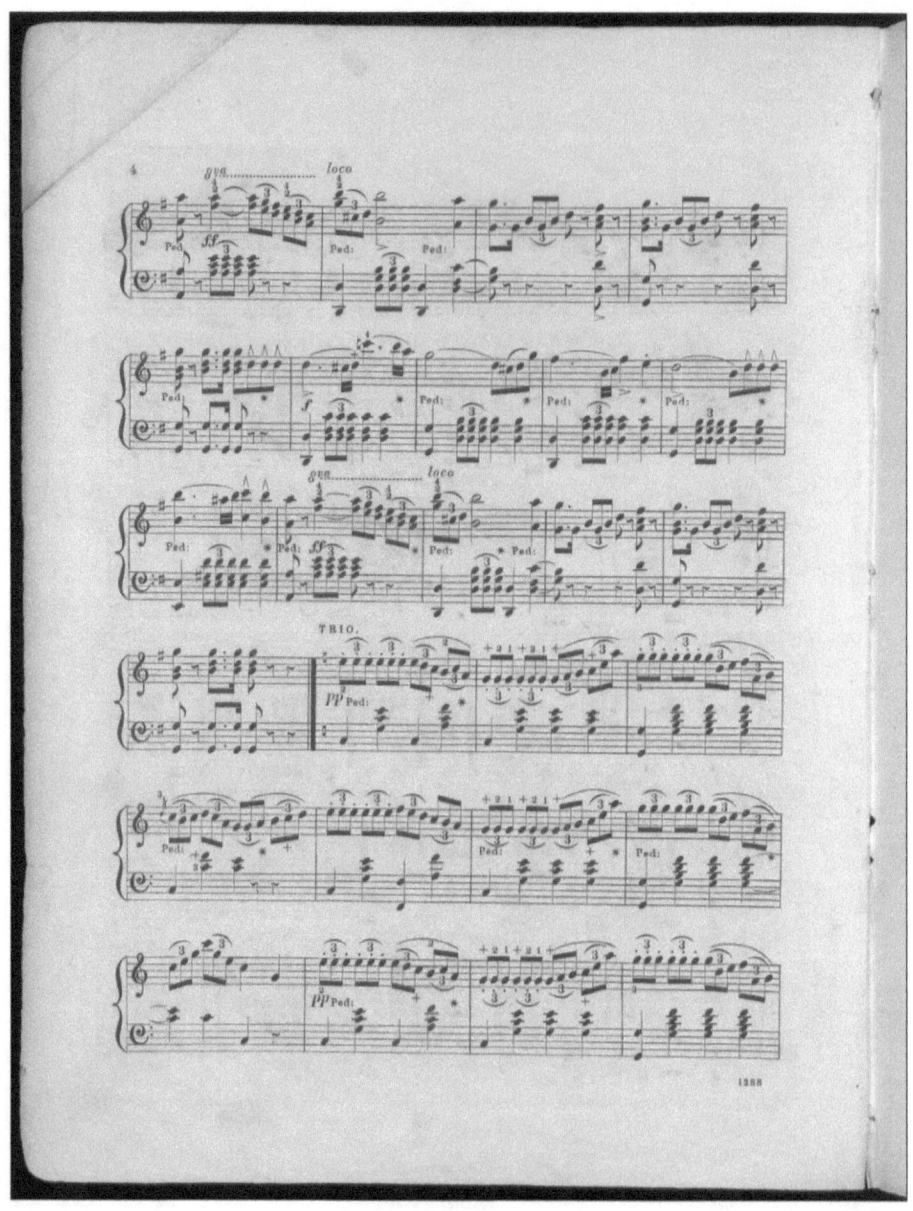

Figure 10: Sheet music for "Col. Doniphan's Grand March."

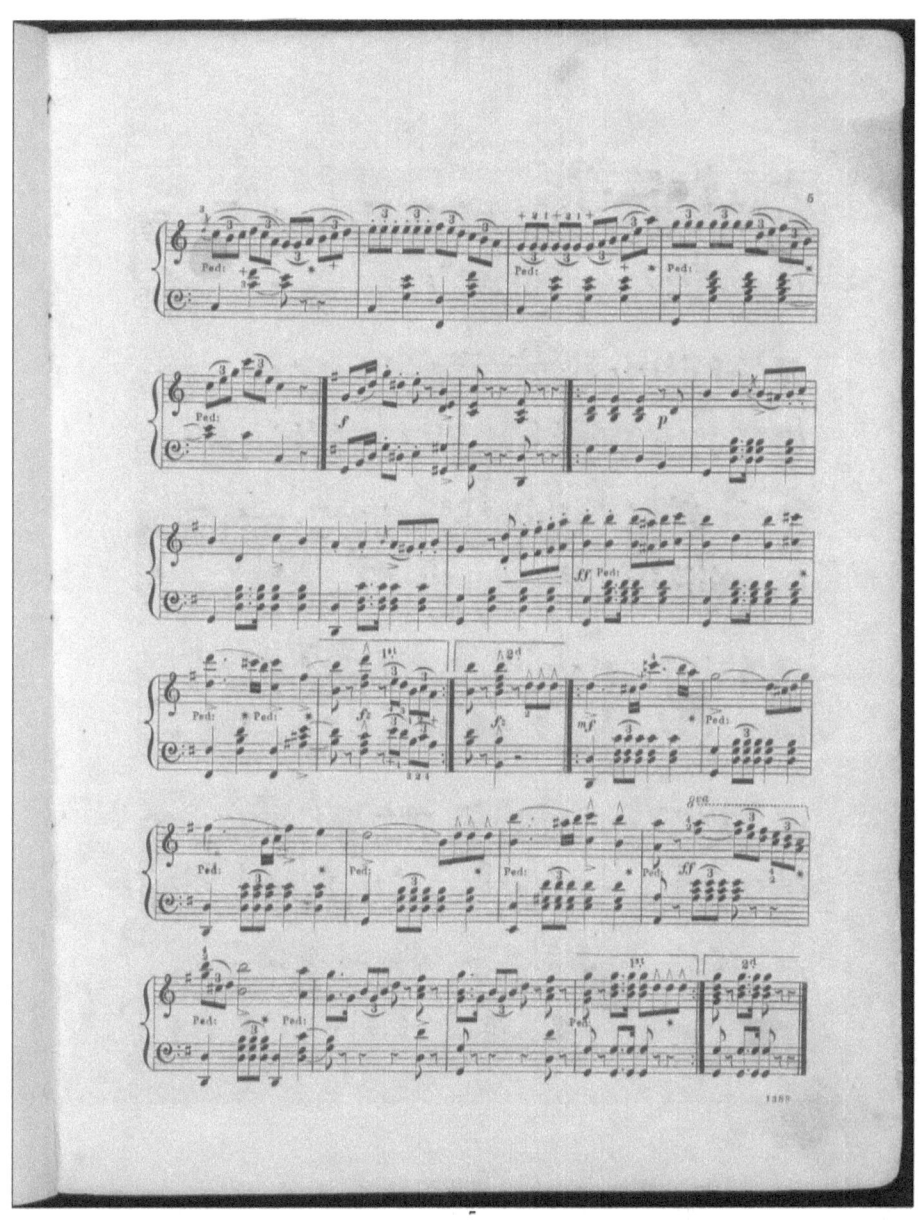

Figure 11: Sheet music for "Col. Doniphan's Grand March."

Figure 12: Portrait of Alexander Doniphan. Earlier in the book the portrait of Alexander Doniphan has been flipped horizontally to fit into the design aesthetic.

Figure 13: Portrait of Elizabeth Thronton Doniphan.

Figure 14: Portrait of Alexander Doniphan, Jr.

Figure 15: A highly stylized lithograph depicting the court martial of the leaders of the Latter-day Saints. This is the full version of this image found earlier in this book.

Figure 16: A 1917-line drawing from the *Kansas City Star* of the Doniphan Statue in Richmond prior to its installaton. This is the full version of this image found earlier in this book.

Figure 17: One of the last portriats of Alexander W. Doniphan, taken in 1878. This is the full version of this image found earlier in this book.

Figure 18: Doniphan - Hubbell House. This is the full version of this image found earlier in this book

Figure 19: Doniphan - Hubbell House historical marker.

Figure 20: Alexander Doniphan Elementary, Liberty, Missouri.

Figure 21: Alexander Doniphan Elementary sign.

Figure 22: Alexander Doniphan Memorial Highway, MO State Hwy 152 from Liberty, Missouri to Levenworth, Kansas.

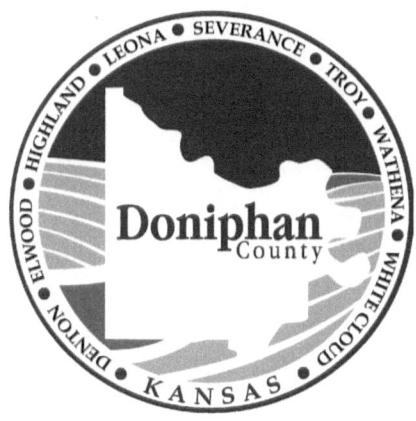

Figure 23: Logo of Doniphan County, Kansas.

IMAGE GALLERY   277

Figure 24: Plaque on the Alexander W. Doniphan Statue in Richmond, Missouri.

Figure 25: Plaque on the Alexander W. Doniphan Statue in Richmond, Missouri.

Figure 26: Plaque on the Alexander W. Doniphan Statue in Richmond, Missouri.

Figure 27: Inscription on the Alexander W. Doniphan Statue in Richmond, Missouri.

ERECTED BY THE STATE OF MISSOURI
IN HONOR OF
COLONEL ALEXANDER W. DONIPHAN
COMMANDER OF FIRST REGIMENT MISSOURI
MOUNTED VOLUNTEERS IN THE WAR WITH MEXICO
BORN MASON COUNTY, KENTUCKY, JULY 9, 1808
DIED RICHMOND, MISSOURI, AUGUST 8, 1887
ON THE ROSTER OF THE GREAT SOLDIERS OF
THE EARTH MUST ALWAYS STAND IN A HALO
OF GLORY THE NAME OF
COLONEL ALEXANDER W. DONIPHAN OF MISSOURI

Figure 28: Inscription on the Alexander W. Doniphan Statue in Richmond, Missouri.

Figure 29: Alexander W. Doniphan statue in Richmond, Missouri.

Figure 30: Alexander W. Doniphan statue in Richmond, Missouri.

Figure 1: *Shoemaker, F. C. (1921). Alexander W. Doniphan, 1806-1887 : Soldier, Lawyer and Orator. In Missouri's Hall of Fame: Lives of Eminent Missourians (p. 107). Columbia, MO: Missouri Book Company.*

Figures 2 & 3: *Missouri Secretary of State - IT. "The Missouri Mormon War." Missouri Secretary of State. Accessed August 10, 2020. https://www.sos.mo.gov/archives/resources/findingaids/miscMormonRecords/eo.*

Figures 4 & 5: *Bond, C. S. (1976). Governor Bond's Rescission order (pp. 1-2) (United States, Missouri, Governor). Jefferson City, MO: Secretary of State. Retrieved August 26, 2020, from https://www.sos.mo.gov/cmsimages/archives/resources/findingaids/miscMormRecs/eo/19760625_RescisOrder.pdfH274   RG5 Secretary of State - Commissions - Executive Orders, July 25 ,1976 (Bond Rescission Order)*

Figure 6: *Currier, N. (1847). The Battle of Sacramento: Fought February 28th 1847 [New York: N. Currier] Photograph found in Popular Graphic Arts, Library of Congress, Washington. Retrieved July, 2020, from https://www.loc.gov/item/90709394/ (Originally photographed 1847)*

Figure 7: *1st Regiment Missouri Volunteers Veterans [Photograph found in Photograph Collection, State Historical Society of Missouri, Columbia]. (1888). Retrieved July, 2020, from https://digital.shsmo.org/digital/collection/imc/id/20296/rec/3 (Doniphan, Alexander W. (Col.). Moss, O.P. (Capt.). Sublett, L.B. (1st Lieut.). Moss, Jas. H.(2nd Lieut.). McCarty, Thos. (1st Sarg.). McClintock, A.K. (2nd Sarg.). Wallis, George H. (Corporal). Groom, Jno. S. Warren, John. Pence, W.H. Campbell)*

Figures 8-11: Sheet music for "Col. Doniphan's Grand March." Figure 8 is the full version of this image found earlier in this book. -- *Waldauer, A., & Beinecke, F. W. (circa 1848). Col. Doniphan's Grand March [Lithograph and sheet music published in St. Louis by Buford & Co.]. Retrieved July, 2020, from Beinecke Rare Book and Manuscript Library, Yale University https://brbl-dl.library.yale.edu/vufind/Record/4087097*

Figure 12: Bingham, G. C. (circa 1850.). Portrait of General Alexander William Doniphan [Unsigned oil painting.]. Retrieved July, 2020, from The State Historical Society of Missouri https://digital.shsmo.org/digital/collection/art/id/356/rec/1

Figure 13: Bingham, G. C. (circa 1850.). Portrait of General Alexander William Doniphan [Unsigned oil painting.]. Retrieved July, 2020, from The State Historical Society of Missouri https://digital.shsmo.org/digital/collection/art/id/356/rec/1

Figure 14: Bingham, G. C. (circa 1850.). Portrait of General Alexander William Doniphan [Unsigned oil painting.]. Retrieved July, 2020, from The State Historical Society of Missouri https://digital.shsmo.org/digital/collection/art/id/356/rec/1

Figure 15: *Carter, C. W. (circa 1885). The Extermination of the Latter Day Saints from the State of Missouri in the Fall of 1838 [Photograph]. Church History Catalog, Church of Jesus Christ of Latter-day Saints, Salt Lake City, UT.*

Figure 16: *A Statue to a Famous Missourian. (1917, January 26). Kansas City Star, p. 7.*

Figure 17: *Garland, R. (1878). Alexander William Doniphan [Three-quarter bust view* *of General Alexander Doniphan b/w photo]. Retrieved July, 2020, from State Historical Society of Missouri https://digital.shsmo.org/digital/collection/imc/id/22094/rec/1*

Figure 18: *Photo Courtesy of Clay County Museum, Liberty, Missouri*

Figure 19: *Photo Courtesy of Giving River Images/Valerie Anderson*

Figures 20 & 21: *Anderson, Valerie. (2020, April 29). Alexander Doniphan Elementry School [Photograph]. Giving River Images, Liberty, MO.*

Figure 22: *Anderson, Valerie. (2020, April 29). Alexander Doniphan Memorial Highway [Photograph]. Giving River Images, Kansas City, MO.*

Figure 23: *Johnson, L. B. (2020, July 16). Doniphan County Logo [Photograph]. Troy, KS.*

Figures 24-28: *Anderson, Valerie. (2020, April 29). Doniphan Statue at the Ray County Courthouse [Photograph]. Giving River Images, Richmond, MO.*

Figures 29 & 30: *Anderson, Valerie. (2020, April 29). Doniphan Statue at the Ray County Courthouse [Photograph]. Giving River Images, Richmond, MO.*

www.ingramcontent.com/pod-product-compliance
Lightning Source LLC
Chambersburg PA
CBHW030146100526
44592CB00009B/151